The
Wednesday
Pen

The
Wednesday
Pen

A Grandfather's Legacy to His Family

Warren R. Higgins
edited by Ris A. Higgins

Brown Books Publishing Group
Dallas, Texas

The Wednesday Pen: A Grandfather's Legacy to His Family

Brown Books Publishing Group
16250 Knoll Trail Drive, Suite 205
Dallas, Texas 75248
www.BrownBooks.com
(972) 381-0009

A New Era in Publishing™

ISBN 978-1-61254-053-5
Library of Congress Control Number 2012939158

Printing in the United States
10 9 8 7 6 5 4 3 2 1

For more information or to contact the author, please go to:
www.TheWednesdayPen.com

Dedicated to my grandson, for what he may have gotten from these notes and for what he has achieved since.

Contents

Acknowledgments

To my dad: I am deeply grateful to you for being willing to share your letters to Ryan. Even now I appreciate the love and discipline you had in writing a letter every week for five years, never missing a week—not one. Thank you for trusting me to publish your stories. They taught Ryan and all of us how to love life and family, how to be a leader in business and the military, how to enjoy sports, and how faith can enrich your life. The longer I live, the more I find of your wisdom in my life.

To my husband, Joe: You are such a good man. Thank you for giving me your time when it was so precious to talk about and finish this book. Your love and support of me during this project helped bring it to life. I love you.

To Ryan and Brandon, my sons: I am so proud of both of you. I can see the impact of Grandpa's stories and letters on the men you have become. You are the reasons I wanted to publish these letters.

To Nance Guilmarten: Thank you. This book would not have seen the light of day without your unwavering support and encouragement.

To Tamara Hall: Thank you for graciously meeting with me and urging me on in every conversation to publish this book.

Preface

The Story of The Wednesday Pen

When my oldest son Ryan turned thirteen, my father was no longer living in Milwaukee where we were, but he still wanted to influence and have an impact on Ryan, his first grandchild, as he entered manhood. He wrote Ryan,

> When you became a teenager, I realized I hadn't been with you or visited with you as much as I wanted. Once when I was lamenting not seeing you, a business associate gave me a pen to use on Wednesdays to write you and share some of my thoughts and experiences with you, since I probably won't be in Milwaukee anymore for the foreseeable future. I kind of thought it was a neat idea. I would prefer being with you and talking and answering questions, but maybe this can be a substitute. This short note format will keep me from "talking" too long, a malady affecting older persons, and my letters won't be too long for you to read them quickly.

And that's how the Wednesday Pen began. Each Wednesday for five years he wrote a letter to Ryan, sharing his experiences and thoughts about life. He never missed a week. Not one. The last Wednesday Pen note was written on August 6, 1997, two days after Ryan's eighteenth birthday. It was my father's way of staying connected with his teenage grandson; little did my father know, he was staying connected with me as well. Each week I laughed or cried or remembered or loved after reading his letter to Ryan. I thought of each one as very precious because they were, and still are, pure Dad.

At first, I saved the letters without knowing what I was going to do with them, but it soon became clear. *The Wednesday Pen: A Grandfather's Legacy to His Family* is an anthology of Higgins traditions, wisdom, and teachings—a legacy to pass on to other grandchildren and great-grandchildren. My brothers, Rob and Charlie, and my sister, Barb, will also laugh and cry and remember and love when they read all the letters. But this is really for the grandchildren: Ryan, Brandon, Samantha, Brian, Chloe, Jess, Jake, and Ian. They will not grow up with this man as their mother or father did, but this collection is the next best thing to learning about the great man who is their grandfather. Space restraints prevented me from including every single letter, which led to this collection that is more focused on life lessons and advice.

It's my father's life—how he has lived it and what he taught us—that is his legacy to his family. What a significant gift he has given us with these letters. Thank you, Dad, for always challenging me to grow, unconditionally loving me, and inspiring my spirit. I love you.

—Ris A. Higgins

Index by Topic

DATE Wednesday 04/20/99

To: Ryan –

MEMORANDUM

DATE Wednesday 04/05/95

To: Ryan –

MEMORANDUM

Can you tell when someone has stolen, lied,
or cheated? In Sunday's homily at Mass,
the priest told a story of an ancient tradition
to ferret out the transgressor. It seems that
the son of a shiekhto be now...

DATE Wednesday 04/19/95

...it" — I'd not heard that
before. Someone was writing

DATE Wednesday 11/16/94

MEMORANDUM

DATE Wednesday 05/03/95

To: Ryan –

MEMORANDUM

Did you know that I graduated from
Paint? Well — not the regular
Paint. It seems that the regular
not use their air field, planes, or
during the winter months, when the
regular classes. They used them, su
only. A bunch of we "aviation"
sent there to make use of the fair
awhile the instructors really lea
They said that the West Pointers

DATE Wednesday 12/22/93

To: Ryan –

MEMORANDUM

Merry Christmas to you — and to
Brandon, your Mom and Joe! We wan
have a "white" Christmas here — hope
that you all have one. Hope, too, that Sa
is good to you this year! Have you been g
good boy? I've been pretty good, so I'
hoping for the best. We got your Mom's

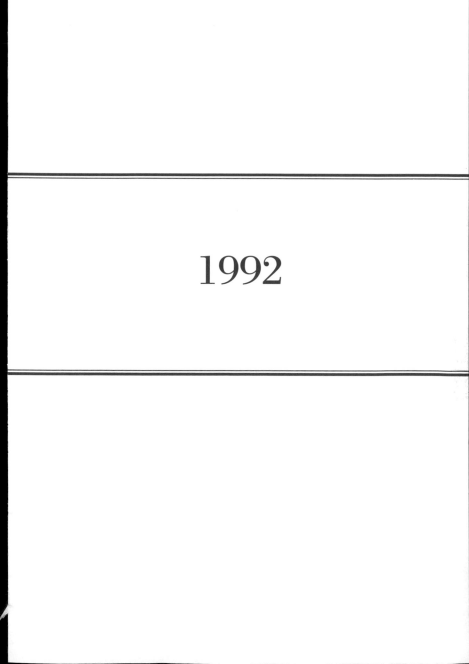

1992

WEDNESDAY, SEPTEMBER 9, 1992

Don't Be One of the Herd

To Ryan:

Thought that I could clear up a quote: "Don't be one of the herd." It should be: "Know when and when not to be one of the herd." You have to be "one of the herd" when it comes to rules, regulations, and laws. "When not to be" is during those times when you put forth that extra effort to excel and do just a little bit more than the other people. That's what got you elected "Mr. President" in sixth grade, Mr. President. I'm looking forward to your other accomplishments. We made raspberry jam today, from our own patch. See you next week.

Love,
Grandpa

PS. Figure I might pen a note to you each week because we're not seeing each other lately.

Free Concert

To Ryan:

It's Wednesday again, and here I am! Grandma and I went to hear the Air Force Academy Band last night. Reminds me of "It ain't what is, but what people thinks it is"—one of my favorite sayings. People thought because it was a free band performance that it wouldn't be any good—so they didn't come. They missed a beauty of a concert. It was awesome and inspiring. It made you feel like you wanted to enlist in the Air Force again. Have you ever thought about trying for an appointment to the Air Force Academy? Remind me to tell you some of my wartime experiences sometime. I've got all kinds of medals to show you. Not worth much, except to me. Played racquetball this morning. Grandma walked. We're both in good shape.

Love,
Grandpa

WEDNESDAY, SEPTEMBER 23, 1992

The Secret of Success

To Ryan:

Years ago your Uncle Rob asked me the secret of my success in the business world. I told him that I wasn't sure just how successful I was. However, if I had been moderately successful it was due to two things:

1. In business, as in life, I always tried to do just a little bit more than was asked or expected of me, sometimes referred to as that "extra mile."
2. Perseverance—that is, to persist or pursue objectives no matter what stands in my way or what difficulties I encounter along the way.

That philosophy got me where I wanted to go, and you know what—it's still with me. Just today they called and told me we'd won four seats to the next Kansas City Chiefs football game here in KC.

Love,
Grandpa

Voting in Elections

To Ryan:

The election seems to be everywhere on the radio, television, and newspapers, doesn't it? In the great democratic form of government that we have in the US, the election will pretty much determine who will lead us for the next four years. I guess that isn't much different from what your school class officers' elections are, though, just on a smaller scale. Do you all vote for someone because he or she is popular, or because you think that they can make a difference in your school? Compare your school election to the nation's election. Who do you think will be our president after November 3? Why do you think that? Who would you vote for? Why do you think Bush, Clinton, and Perot want to be president? Would you want to be president? Why?

Love,
Grandpa

WEDNESDAY, OCTOBER 21, 1992

Learn to Ask Questions

To Ryan:

One of the most important things I learned during my time in the Army was to ask questions. I carried that idea through college and in my whole career. A little poem has always helped remind me:

> *I have six honest serving men*
> *They taught me all I know,*
> *Their names are who and what and why*
> *And where and when and how!*

Starting my questions with one of these six will get responses with lots of information. Check your newspaper articles. The first paragraph should always answer all six of these questions. As a high school newspaper reporter and college engineering magazine associate editor, I checked myself out on every article I wrote just that way. You may want to use that to write reports, too.

Love,
Grandpa

Sales Technique

To Ryan:

What kind of a brilliant start could I write to begin this note? That's what I've been thinking about. Reason, you might ask? Well, I wanted to get across a sales technique that I learned many years ago, at the start of my career. It can be used in a letter, a conversation, a report, or any kind of presentation, Mr. President. It's all wrapped up in three words: Star, Chain, Hook. The star is the first idea. It gets the attention of the reader or listener. The chain is the connecting idea or facts of the project. The hook is the clincher, request, or main point of the communication. Use the three words to plan your presentations! Watch how others use it to sell themselves, ideas, or projects.

Love,
Grandpa

WEDNESDAY, NOVEMBER 4, 1992

What Would Grandpa Do?

To Ryan:

Whenever I give a presentation or speech, I like to have something for my audience to remember. Similarly, when I listen, I like to take away something significant. Recently, our priest gave a short sermon that really impressed me. His hook was "What would Jesus do?" He suggested that whenever you had a decision to make regarding some action you were about to do, if you were in a quandary, to just say to yourself, "What would Jesus do?" It's interesting, it's fun, and it certainly leads me to do the right thing. You know, it's hard for me to forget those four words! But I guess, as something more down to earth for you, let me challenge you to try to forget these four words: "What would Grandpa do?" Carry me with you in all you do, in school (I'm especially good in math and English), at play, and when you're awake or asleep.

Love,

Grandpa

First Solo Flight

To Ryan:

Veteran's Day! It reminds me of my Air Force experience during World War II. We were shot at many times during bombing runs over Japan. However, I probably remember the time I almost killed myself during flight training more than anything. It was on my first solo flight. We were in Bennettsville, South Carolina, flying PT-17s—yellow, single-engine biplanes. I was coming in for my first solo landing. There were tall pine trees lining the airfield. I kept pulling back on the stick trying to get over the tall trees by raising the nose of the plane "just a little higher." Suddenly, I felt the plane shudder as it was about to stall out. Fortunately, I recovered in time to ram the throttle forward and power the engine over the trees. I really sweated that one out.

Love,
Grandpa

WEDNESDAY, DECEMBER 9, 1992

St. Anthony

To Ryan:

Well, he did it again! Who did what, you might ask? About a week before we left for Florida, I was getting prepared. Since I had difficulty getting two-dollar bills in Florida in the past, I went to the bank and got $200 worth of $2s in a bundle. On other errands, I "stashed" the package in an envelope and put it in the car's trash bag. Wouldn't you know, I forgot to take it out when I got home. Subsequently, Grandma went out for errands. She got the car washed, including cleaning out the inside. About an hour later, I started missing my $2 bills. St. Anthony is the patron saint for lost things and loss recovery. So, I said a little prayer to St. Anthony and asked him to help me find the lost $2 bills. They weren't in the car! Where were they? Happy ending! I went to the car wash and the manager retrieved the money from their trash barrel. St. Anthony did it again!

Love,
Grandpa

Saying "No"

To Ryan:

Want to hear a story about your mom? OK! When she was about your age, a teenager, we were talking about weekend activities. She had invitations for two parties. We were about to say, "All right, but with certain conditions," when she said, "I don't think that I should be allowed to go to both parties." We said, "All right, you can't go to both! You can choose which one to go to yourself." She did. Later, we overheard Rob talking to your mom. He asked if she was going to that certain party. Your mom replied, "No, Mom and Dad won't let me!" How about that? But you know, I did the very same thing as a teenager. Friends wanted me to drive, after I'd driven a number of times before. Rather than them taking advantage of me, and our car's availability, I said, "No, my folks won't let me!" Perhaps both your mom and I used our respective parents to help us solve our own dilemma of peer pressure versus good conduct and good sense. Not a bad idea, though, to use once in a while.

Love,
Grandpa

Pearl Harbor Christmas Tree

To Ryan:

Merry Christmas! So wish that Grandma and I could be with you for the big day. We'll be talking to you, though—along with all the rest of the Higgins tribe—tonight, with you all celebrating together at Aunt Karen and Uncle Charlie's. Uncle Rob is here with us in Florida, so we'll all be together in two groups talking to each other. Christmas and Uncle Rob reminds me of a family story. One night, when we were living in Zanesville, Ohio, I stumbled over something on the floor of the darkened living room as I walked through. It was Uncle Rob lying on the floor, head resting in his cupped hands. He was entranced with the beautiful lighted Christmas tree. When asked what he was doing there, he said, "The tree is so great and it's only up for such a short time that I want to enjoy it for as long as I can!" Well, following that episode, Grandma and all the kids and I decided to put up and trim the Higgins Christmas tree on the Sunday closest to Pearl Harbor Day, December 7. Grandma also remembered she had been trimming her tree on December 7, 1941.

Love,
Grandpa

New Year's Resolutions

To Ryan:

Well, Christmas is over. We sang Happy Birthday to Jesus over a birthday candle on Christmas. After all, there wouldn't be a Christmas without Jesus's birthday, would there? Now is the time for New Year's Eve celebrating, and also for making resolutions for 1993. I can remember one New Year's resolution when I was a subteen. A bunch of us had smoked "butts" of cigarettes during the year before. That New Year's Eve, resolution number one for me was to give up smoking for the year ahead. And do you know that I have never smoked since then? I was way before the present-day trends on "no smoking." Did I miss anything? No. Anymore, I try to think up resolutions to make me a better person, a better husband, a better father, a better grandfather, a better citizen of the United States and the world, and a better Christian. Resolutions are to build character, not to be a character. Character—that's doing the right thing, in the right way, at the right time, in the right place, for the right reason, for the right people. Happy New Year!

Love,
Grandpa

DATE Wednesday 01/11/95

To: Ryan —

DATE Wednesday 03/22/95

To: Ryan —

MEMORANDUM

How much do you read the newspaper? Our
next door neighbor doesn't get a paper. I think
that she (a single mother with a seven year old)
probably is so busy and possibly feels that she
gets enough news also TV. Cause she
doesn't have...

DATE Wednesday 01/26/9_

! Of course I'm interested! Who
...

MEMORANDUM

DATE Wednesday 03/15/95

MEMORANDUM
Patrick —

DATE Wednesday 12/15/93

To: Ryan —

MEMORANDUM

Wow! Congratulations on your ___
wrestling award ___ great preparation
and ___ were awarded you ___
and strength were awarded you ___
you've heard of body ___ I'm
you know what messages you send ___
body positioning of arms legs ___
sure to think of ___ your body language
... wrestling match tells your opponent
going to have some kind of match
a new one though ...

DATE Wednesday 12/29/93

To: Ryan —

MEMORANDUM

Christmas has been ___ Christmas has you
"What did you get for Christmas?" Our
neighbors, when we lived in Ohio, had children
the same ages as your Mom, Uncle Rob, Uncle ___
and Aunt Barb. Bill Greene, Rob's buddy
next door came over to compare gifts. He asked
Uncle Rob the same question we heard the ___
question. Rob really had trouble answering ___
... Bill, on the other ___

1993

WEDNESDAY, JANUARY 6, 1993

Being a Paperboy

To Ryan:

Did you get your Christmas present of the book on teenage jobs? How'd you like it? Or maybe you haven't had a chance to read it. We thought it might give you some good ideas. What a background for the author, but no more than I think you are capable of, Mr. President. You know that, as a young man in grade school, I had a paper route for the Milwaukee Journal. After school everyday, I'd pick up anywhere from thirty to sixty papers at the green paperboy shack on Greenfield Avenue and peddle papers to my customers. I had three different routes over a period of two or three years. My dad would get up some cold, wintry Sunday mornings to help me. Those Sunday papers were big and heavy with advertising in those days, too. Daily, I'd carry all my papers about a mile. Most fun was on Saturday, when I'd collect for the week's papers! 'Course, at Christmas, paperboys would expect—and usually get—an extra tip for the holidays. You really get a picture of people, their values, their outlook, their generosity, and their compassion as a paperboy. Too bad they don't have paperboys anymore.

Love,
Grandpa

Making Decisions

To Ryan:

Are you ready for a new president, Mr. President? A week from today, Clinton will be installed as our new president. That got me to thinking about leaders and leadership. While we were walking the beach this morning, I formulated my ideas. To be a leader, a person must accumulate the facts to the best of his or her ability, make a decision based on those facts and their own experience, and be prepared to accept the responsibilities of that decision. You would be amazed at the number of people that are unwilling and cannot make a decision, or are willing or able to accept the consequences. During my career, in about every manager's job I had, people worked for me that were older, had more experience, were smarter, and had more seniority with the company, but they didn't have the job I had because of a lack of leadership. It was principally because they wouldn't make a decision and stand by it. You can do it. You are a leader in the making.

Love,
Grandpa

WEDNESDAY, JANUARY 27, 1993

Who Are You?

To Ryan:

Some years ago, a friend of ours came up to me and said, "Who are you?" Well, he knew me well enough not to have to ask that question. He was making a point to me. He said to imagine someone coming up to me and asking that question. With no reason to question his asking me the question, "Answer it," my friend said. "Answer it with three statements, and there are no perfect answers." Well, as most people do, I gave my name first, the fact that I was married and had four children second, and that I was employed at Allis-Chalmers third. He said the best answer (for anyone) was: First, "I'm a child of God"; second, the person's own name; and third, the names of his wife and children. Actually, it's sort of a simplified test of what a person considers the most important things in their life. Best answer would probably be 1) God, 2) Self, and 3) Family. You'd be surprised at how many people say, "I'm president of my club," or, "I'm manager of the store," or, "I'm a war veteran," or, "I'm star of the team," or, "I've lived in their city for thirty years at such 'n such address." By the way, Ryan, who are you?

Love,
Grandpa

Forming Habits

To Ryan:

Did you ever hear the expression "a creature of habit"? Or "that's habit forming"? Or "get into the habit of doing something a certain way"? 'Course, there are good habits and bad habits. I was going to write this note left-handed, but I figured it might take too long. But I could do it. I have a right-handed habit; it's something I do the same way all the time without thinking. Think about habits. For instance, I'll bet you, like 99 percent of all people, cut off the top of a piece of pie when you eat it, instead of starting at the crust end. Watch other people do the same thing. Like, as a matter of habit, I brush my teeth first thing each morning, before I shave, wash my face, or comb my hair. Occasionally, I change my habit of doing something just for the heck of it, to do something different for a change. When I develop a bad habit, I consciously change to a good one because I follow the Roman emperor and philosopher, Marcus Aurelius, who said, "Act the way you want to be and soon you will be the way you act!"

Love,
Grandpa

WEDNESDAY, FEBRUARY 10, 1993

Alternative Plans

To Ryan:

During my working career my staff used to kid me, saying that my middle initial should be A. A for alternative, that is. I guess that I would always ask them for an alternative plan to any proposal. That was supposed to help them if anything went wrong with their original proposal. Also, it was to alert them to the realization that there are many ways to reach an objective. In college I learned that in machine design courses there are alternatives to any design to do a job. For instance, say you want to go to Kansas City from Milwaukee. For speed, you can fly, but it costs a lot. For less cost you can go by train. For even less cost you can go by bus. For personal convenience, you can go by car at even less cost. The ultimate lowest cost is to go by foot and walk. That's the least cost and most time. 'Course, there are many reasons besides time and money to decide on a plan and form alternatives. Think about that!

Love,
Grandpa

Anticipation

To Ryan:

When your Uncle Rob was in college, he worked at the company where I worked, so he and I would drive to work together each day. To make it interesting, we would alternate driving. To make it even more interesting, and as a bit of competition, we would play a "brake game." Actually, it was a game of anticipation. We counted the number of times that the driver had to touch the brake pedal for the trip from Whitefish Bay to Cudahy before there were any expressways. It meant timing your speed, positioning in traffic and relationship to oncoming traffic, checking out stop and go lights, and careful driving. In a word, it was anticipation of all facets in driving a car, much like the steelworker walking on the structural girders high in the building skeleton. When asked how he managed to survive in such a dangerous job, he said, "Anticipation. I anticipate what I would do if the worst thing happened after each step." Think about it.

Love,
Grandpa

WEDNESDAY, FEBRUARY 24, 1993

Taking the Job No One Wants

To Ryan:

You've played Little League or Biddy League baseball at third base. Well, your Uncle Rob played Biddy League Football when he was young. I asked him what position he wanted to play when he signed up. He thought quarterback or pass-catching end would be great! Instead, I suggested that he try out for center. He'd get his hands on the ball on every play and he'd be right in the middle of every play. Also, he'd have little or no competition, 'cause no one else wanted to be center and get their face pushed in the mud and be under every pileup. It's like being catcher on a baseball team, using the "tools of ignorance." I guess that I have always advocated volunteering particularly for "taking the job that no one else wants." It's really fun; you have little or no competition, you generally get bigger and better rewards, and you get great self-satisfaction doing something others can't or don't want to do!

Love,
Grandpa

First Impressions

To Ryan:

What are your first recollections of your Grandma Higgins? What were your first impressions of me? The first impression that a person has about other persons, places, and things tends to be a long-lasting image, sometimes difficult to change, for better or worse.

That's one reason that I always tried—and still try—to make a good impression for myself when I meet someone. That goes for my preparation and presentation of a project to my boss when I was still working. It paid off for me. I guess that's why Grandma always wants the house to look nice for visitors, especially first-time visitors. How about you and your first impressions? Which brings up a point— I'm always learning. Lately, I learned or realized something when talking to Samantha, your cousin. To keep her from a simple yes or no answer, to get her to talk more to us, I realized that if I used our famous six words (who, what, when, where, why, and how) to start my questions to her, she'd have to talk other than yes or no.

Love,
Grandpa

WEDNESDAY, MARCH 10, 1993

Capturing Ideas at Night

To Ryan:

About every morning around four or five o'clock, I have my twilight time. It's not like the weird TV show of some years ago. My twilight time is my time for ideas. Used to be that it would bother me when I'd wake up at night. But my mom told me not to worry, that just resting in bed was enough for my body to rejuvenate itself for the upcoming day. After that, no more worry problems on my part. Instead, I used the time to fantasize, dream, plan, and just plain think. Also, used to be that when I'd awaken earlier in the evening, I'd get some great ideas—but I couldn't go back to sleep for fear of not remembering the ideas for the next day. My mom solved the worry problem—I came up with the solution to forgetting great ideas. Thereafter, and to this day (or night) I have a pencil and paper next to my bed every night. I write down my ideas and go back to sleep knowing my ideas are secure for the morrow. But often I "feed" on my ideas during twilight time. Guess where I get all my themes for my notes to you!

Love,
Grandpa

Lessons from the Military

To Ryan:

Down in Florida, we meet a lot of retirees. Since we are so close to Patrick Air Force Base, a lot of the retirees live nearby. At times I've thought about what my career and life would have been had I stayed in the Air Force after the Second World War. What officer rank would I have attained? Would I have flown in Korea and Vietnam? Where would we have been stationed during the years I would have been in the service? However, I'm not looking back. We did all right for ourselves, so I just am happy that I learned as much as I did during the three years that I "fought" the war. What did I learn? Well, obviously I learned to fly multi-engine planes. Probably more importantly, since I haven't piloted a plane since then, I learned to ask questions at school, at work, and at home. Also, I learned to organize myself and my work, and I learned orderliness in my physical surroundings. Surprisingly, those four things are the essence.

Love,
Grandpa

WEDNESDAY, APRIL 7, 1993

Being Grandpa's Stockbroker

To Ryan:

So good to see you personally again. We get together so seldom. We are looking forward to the first week in May, when we'll be with you and Brandon for a week! Grandma and I are really looking forward to it. It was interesting talking about your working or having a job. I guess none of the ideas from that book I gave you at Christmas struck a chord. That book was written by a former teenager with bountiful ideas. Here's one that may tickle your fancy: How'd you like to be my "stockbroker"? This would take a lot of intelligence (which you have), experience (which I could share with you—and you're a quick learner), time (you can always find time, if you are really interested in something), money (which I could supply and control), decision making (not too difficult when you have the facts), follow-up (a necessary characteristic for any good business plan or money making venture), and luck (because no one can completely control the market). To begin: read page 87 in the April 1993 issue of Reader's Digest. Seventh graders!

Love,

Grandpa

Being Grandpa's Stockbroker

To Ryan:

Well, to continue with what I wrote about last week, I misspoke—or rather, miswrote. A stockbroker is a person who executes orders for others to buy and sell stock. I should have asked if you want to be my stockbroker. That is, for you to research companies to determine whether or not you could find a company that is growing, making money, has good products or services, treats customers and employees well, and looks to being successful in the future. That type of company is one that a person would invest their hard-earned money in with the anticipation of earning a return of growth in the price of the stock, as well as in dividends. But then again, you might not be interested in something like that right now, even though we'd split the money we made over the amount of our investment. So tomorrow is income tax day! Do you realize that we all have to support our government operations with about a quarter of all the money we earn? Thank goodness I've paid taxes for forty years because I've had a job and earned money to pay them. Think about it.

Love,
Grandpa

Becoming a Pilot

To Ryan:

Do you like to fly? I went into the World War II scene wanting to fly. When I was young, I built model airplanes out of balsa wood from a kit. My brother Chuck already had graduated as an Air Force pilot, and I thought that when I went to war I wanted to come back whole or not at all. So I signed up with the Army Air Corps, not the Air Force! They called me up while I was a freshman at Cornell. We were all excited. After a few orientation flights, I felt sick, literally. They "washed out" cadets who got sick, so I was really worried. I called up Chuck, who had graduated as a cadet three years earlier, gotten his "wings," and was flying for Pan American Airways out of Miami. He said to chew gum. So, in primary flying school, I bought a box of Dentine chewing gum. Before each flight, I stuck a stick of gum in my mouth. About a month later, my instructor called my name. I reached in my flying suit for my gum. I had forgotten my gum! I about panicked. But I went ahead and flew without it. No problem! I never had to chew gum again.

Love,
Grandpa

Short and Sweet

To Ryan:

It was so good being with you last week. We really enjoyed it, though we didn't get as much time to talk as I would have liked. On the other hand, Grandma chides me on talking too much. That's why I pen these notes to you on short memo pads. That way I can't "talk" too much. I'm sure that you prefer the notes short and sweet, too. Have you noticed anything different? All my sentences have been short. They are about ten to fifteen words long. Did you go back and count? I did. While I don't always follow the rule, years ago, a teacher drilled it into me. "Keep your thoughts and sentences short and to the point," she'd say. You keep your reader from being confused. You keep from rambling pointlessly. People are more attentive. They "listen." Long ago, I realized that it was much harder to write and deliver a short speech. Think about it. Check your latest school reports.

Love,
Grandpa

New Time System

To Ryan:

I'm sure that you have studied the metric system in math or science in school already. We in the USA use the inch-pound system of measurement, but 90 percent of the rest of the world uses the metric system for measurements of weights, length, and distance. Ours is really an archaic system; theirs is much simpler to use. So guess what: your grandfather has invented a metric time system! All the world (100 percent) uses the second-minutes-hour system to measure time. My system is the Tik-Tok Time System. The day is divided into ten divisions called tiks. The tenth of every day is further divided into ten more divisions called decitiks. Each decitik is further divided into ten more divisions called centitiks. On the other hand, ten tiks are a dekatik; and ten dekatiks, or one hundred tiks, are a hectotik. Noon is at five tik; midnight at ten tik. An instrument to measure tik time is called a tok, instead of a clock. So, noon is five o'tok, midnight is ten o'tok. Think about it. School is 3.3 tiks long, not eight hours.

Love,
Grandpa

National Honor Society

To Ryan:

I'm sure that you have heard of the National Honor Society in high school. Did you know that your mom and dad were in NHS? And also Uncle Rob, Uncle Charlie, and Aunt Barb? And Grandma, too? But ole Grandpa never made it. I was robbed! Truth of the matter is that I didn't make it. It was tough because I was the reporter assigned to the story both as a junior and as a senior. It meant a lot to get it, or, in my case, not to get it. I took my solace in the fact that I was the only one in my class to get two college scholarships, and one of about only six to get any scholarship at all. But as you can see, I still remember that from high school. It was a great disappointment. If you are really in earnest about Annapolis and the Navy Seals, you will probably get good grades in high school, get into extracurricular activities, and make the National Honor Society, too. Good luck, good study habits, and good perseverance in all your school activities.

Love,
Grandpa

Do It Now

To Ryan:

While writing this note, I'm looking at a desk letter holder that has emblazoned across the front of it: *Do It Now.* That's a good reminder for me. I guess that we all tend to procrastinate, putting things off until later. The trouble is that oftentimes I forget what it was I was supposed to do. That's embarrassing! Has that happened to you, too? Actually, I have a good reminder-er, your grandma. I expect your mom helps you along the same. I say "helps" because that's a better way of saying it than "nags." Nonetheless, when I "do it now," whatever the task, I feel a lot better with a feeling of accomplishment. Then, on to the next. When I was still working at Allis-Chalmers, I'd try to start the day by mentally lining up the projects with my "jobs to do today" list. If possible, I'd put the most onerous task first, to "do it now," and get it over with. Think about it!

Love,
Grandpa

Write It Down

To Ryan:

Perhaps it doesn't apply to teenagers, but early on I learned to "write it down." Nowadays it's good for me to write notes to myself as reminders to do something, lest I forget. 'Course, we talked about the notepad beside the bed, writing down an idea that pops up during the night so as not to forget it in the morn and allow sleep during the night. I've found that "writing it down" during a meeting with customers, suppliers, or fellow employees was always a good idea. Everyone knew that I was making notes, so it kept us all honest, straightforward, and brief. During contract negotiations with the unions, I'd write down all the jokes that were told, so that I could tell Grandma that night. I had a terrible memory. Still have a poor one. "Write it down" has to be a good idea for you coming into high school this fall. You'll be besieged with dates, times, and lessons. Think about it.

Love,
Grandpa

WEDNESDAY, JUNE 16, 1993

The Death of a Comrade

To Ryan:

We had some sad news today. Ed Allgot, our right-side waist gunner on our B-29 crew during World War II, died of bone cancer in New York. A bombing crew has a special feeling for each other. We became almost like brothers. Each crew member had a job to do. All our lives depended on each doing his job well. I flew twenty-one missions over Japan as a pilot, one more as airplane commander. It was with two different crews, the Lucky Strike and the Reamatroid. Ed was on the second crew. We had some great experiences. One time, we had replaced an engine and were breaking it in. That meant flying around Tinian just putting hours of usage on the engine. We noticed a B-24 plane below us up ahead. For fun, as a joke, we feathered (that is, stopped) the two engines on the left side. We revved up the two engines on the right side. Then we put our plane in a power glide, catching up to the B-24 on its right side. We leveled off at the same altitude and, with our accumulated speed, passed the B-24 with the other pilot with his feet up on the steering column waving while I flew!

Love,
Grandpa

Getting into a Service Academy

To Ryan:

Yesterday, the local paper featured an article about a student who had been awarded two appointments to US Service Academies. In this case, it was Annapolis and the Coast Guard Academy. The student had decided to accept the Coast Guard appointment. (Did you know that your grandpa had received two scholarships, one to Cornell and one to Lehigh University?) Anyway, I immediately became interested because of you. The student had met with a guidance counselor first thing upon entering the local high school four years ago. All classes, including electives and extracurricular activities, were directed to accomplishing the goal of getting an appointment. It worked. In fact, twofold. I think that the Coast Guard might be easier to get into, but what the heck, you can get into the Seals from either school. Can you imagine, the son of some local friends of ours turned down an appointment because it wasn't the one he wanted, even though the results would have been about the same? Think about it.

Love,
Grandpa

What to Take in a Flood

To Ryan:

Grandma and I went out gawking again at the disastrous flooding from the Missouri River. ("Disastrous" didn't look right, so I looked it up in my ever-present dictionary and corrected it!) Anyway, people are evacuating everywhere that is likely to flood. They're taking their prized possessions only. It got me thinking, if we were in a situation where we could only take, say, five possessions, what would we take? How about you? It would be tough. Would a person take the monetary or expensive items, the personal, emotional family items, or the seemingly irreplaceable items? For us, it would be:

1. Our loose-leaf binder with all our financial data
2. Our photo albums with pics of all our children, grandchildren, other relatives, and friends
3. Valuable paintings by my mom and famous artists
4. Precise electronic and electric equipment that would be hard and expensive to replace
5. Anything else that water would permanently destroy

What would you take? Think about it.

Love,
Grandpa

Memory and Intelligence

To Ryan:

Memory is a great attribute. It seems as though everyone these days looks at older guys such as me and shakes their head. They think that older people are so forgetful. 'Course, look at all the things that a person has to remember as age comes on. I'll bet that you have some instances where you can't remember. Yet you're only a fifth as old as I am! I've got a pet theory on memory. I think that memory is the principal characteristic of intelligence. Logic and common sense, combined with memory, make for an intelligent person. Example: If you have a problem and you can remember various solutions that you read or were taught, combined with logic on the application or use, coupled with common sense, you have an intelligent answer. If you have a math or science test and can remember from previous lessons, you can select the logical answer. Does all that make sense? Think about it.

Love,
Grandpa

WEDNESDAY, AUGUST 4, 1993

Enjoying High School

To Ryan:

Happy birthday to you, happy birthday to you, happy birthday dear Ryan, happy birthday to you! Wow—it seems like such a short time ago that you became a teenager! Enjoy! Wasn't it interesting that night that you and I went to your high school orientation meeting? On the way, we talked about your next four years in high school. I commented that you should really enjoy these four years especially. It seems that most people agree that a person generally makes and keeps the best friends during one's high school years. Then, the movie that we saw that night emphasized exactly the same thought—enjoy your high school years, you'll look back as their being the best four years of your life. Pick good friends, study hard, and do your best in academics, sports, and socially. Enjoy them all.

Love,
Grandpa

"You be nice to dogs . . ."

To Ryan:

Your Uncle Charlie is good for a couple stories. When he was yet a young lad, maybe about Brandon's age, he had a couple of scenarios that I have repeated and used many times since. I don't remember exactly the circumstance, but I well remember the words of the first instance. We must have warned him about possible problems with getting too friendly with strange dogs. He commented, "You be nice to dogs, and they'll be nice to you." 'Course, it's true with humans, too. Animals and people respond to you in kind—be nice and they're nice; be nasty and they can be mighty nasty, too. Sure, you can find instances to contradict that proposition, but they are rare cases. In those deals, a retort diametrically opposite to that proffered, you ignore it, walk away from it, or try again, as suits the occasion. Uncle Charlie's second story next week!

Love,
Grandpa

WEDNESDAY, AUGUST 18, 1993

Finishing Big Jobs

To Ryan:

Uncle Charlie's other story, referred to last week, has to do with his job philosophy. He really bugged us to let him cut the grass back in Zanesville, Ohio. Your mom and Uncle Rob had the job, alternating the mowing and raking in the front yard and the backyard. They each got ten cents for the job each week. Can you imagine cutting the grass for a dime a week? Our lawn was larger than yours is on Laurel Court. Well, we finally said, "OK, you can take over for Rob." We watched him cut the backyard. It was about half an acre. Instead of a long run down one side, he proceeded to cut a small patch about fifteen feet by fifteen feet. After finishing one little patch square, he'd mow another small square. When I questioned him, he said, "The big backyard looked overwhelming at first glance. So I figured that I'd cut a small piece, get it done, and start another. Before I knew it, the whole yard was cut and done." Big jobs can be completed a little at a time. Think about it.

Love,
Grandpa

Accomplishments

To Ryan:

Congratulations again on the making of the freshman team, and even more importantly to you being named first-string wide receiver! You really worked hard, I'm sure, in getting this spot. Wow, now you've got a load on your back to keep it, eh? I've got a favorite philosophy relative to accomplishments, awards, and travels. I get a third of my total pleasure in preparing and working toward my goal or trip. A second third comes in actually getting, doing, or traveling. The last third is the afterglow, the reflecting and talking about it when all is over. I know you are enjoying the first third now. Enjoy it! Your second third is ahead of you. Work at it and have fun, doing it the best that you can. Turn that anticipation motivation into hard blocking, tackling, and catching passes. By the by, I found the blowgun. It's yours!

Love,
Grandpa

"Taste-Test"

To Ryan:

School days, school days, good ole-fashioned rule days; reading, and writing, and arithmetic; taught to the tune of a hickory stick—there's that singing again! Well, you're back to school, high school! I'll bet that you're really going to enjoy it. Do enjoy. The next four years will be wonderful, full of fun and excitement. But, back to "rules": I always liked to "taste-test" things. No, not always, because I developed it later, but I pass it on to you for use because it helped me over the years, keeping me from major embarrassment. Now, that's not literally taste, just figuratively speaking, to see if data, decisions, or results were "in the ballpark." If something didn't taste right—that is, if it didn't seem logical or reasonable—I'd question myself, my calculations, my assumptions, or even other people's input, and rethink the situation. That was, and still is, my taste-test rule. Think about it.

Love,
Grandpa

Being Stranded on an Island

To Ryan:

Remember a couple weeks ago we "talked" about the five items that you would rescue from your home if it was being flooded? Well, Grandma and I are going to Florida again this winter and we're deciding what to take. The first time, about seven years ago, we took way too much. We never wore many clothes that we took. Each year we've cut down to "base necessities." It got me thinking about an interesting scenario. If a person was about to be stranded on a desert island in the Pacific Ocean, and was allowed to take five items (say, from a fully stocked ocean liner), what should be taken? It would be fun for a group of people to put their choices down on a piece of paper and then compare. My choices, you ask? Well, let's see . . .

1. A big box of matches because there's no electricity there
2. A large, sharp knife
3. A large spool of strong fishing line
4. A Bible
5. A set of clothes including hat, shirt, pants, and shoes

What would you take? Think about it.

Love,
Grandpa

WEDNESDAY, OCTOBER 6, 1993

Teamwork in the Military

To Ryan:

There was an article in the paper today about a flight crewmember, a navigator, who was recalling his World War II missions and his crew. He had searched around the country for them. He felt like they were his long lost brothers. He related about facing combat and the enemy together. It drew them ever closer. I knew just what he was talking about. It happened to me. The eleven members of my crew were—and still are—like brothers or family to me. We worked as a team because our very lives depended on it at times. We were successful because of our teamwork, we accomplished our missions, and all came home well and happy. It's good that you're experiencing teams and teamwork now, especially in sports. There are a lot of parallels. Think about it.

Love,
Grandpa

Dealing with Success

To Ryan:

Congratulations! You are in some pretty "heady" territory! Your kickoff return and intercepted pass return has family, teammates, and friends going ga-ga over you, I'm sure. It's a time of learning for you now, learning how to deal with success. A lot has been written about dealing with failure— "keep the stiff upper lip," "there will be another time," or "there's not a loser in this locker room." It's probably as difficult, if not more so, to deal effectively with success. The individual, or the team, doesn't want to get obnoxiously cocky or disdainfully superior, yet one does want to revel in accomplishment. I guess I've always felt an inner satisfaction in situations like that. I knew I'd "done good," and it saved disparaging remarks if I screwed up next time!

Love,

Grandpa

The Stickmen

To Ryan:

I'd say that I'm probably an average person. I've worked hard and persistently to the best of my ability at the time. I say that because I'm probably a better athlete now than I was in my teens. Do you know that I never earned a letter in high school? I went out for football, basketball, volleyball, and wrestling. I was too slow for anything in track. It was fun. My friends were all jocks. Matter of fact, a bunch of us who were cut from varsity basketball went out to Country Day School and beat their varsity. We had a ball and called ourselves "The Stickmen," all tall and skinny! Fortunately, we all studied, enjoyed school, and got good grades. Our crowd, the jocks, included non-jocks, like even Bill Rehnquist, now chief justice of the US Supreme Court. We were all just a bunch of average guys.

Love,
Grandpa

Great-Grandpa's Character

To Ryan:

You didn't have the opportunity to meet your great-grandfather, my father, Edward F. Higgins. I remember him vividly, of course. When I was a teenager, I would become embarrassed because of him. That is, he had the characteristic of talking to everyone, strangers and friends alike. Not only that, but he'd tell about my latest exploits, accomplishments, and awards or honors. That would embarrass me. Because I loved him, I endured it. Years passed. One day I met an old friend of the family. He asked about Dad. He said that since Mom and Dad had moved to Florida, he really missed him and his charm. He then went on about how much he enjoyed my dad, his vitality, his enthusiasm, and his talking. I guess that I really hadn't appreciated the impression my dad made on people. I realized that people loved him. He was a character, but a lovable character. It made such an impression on me that I have emulated him, and I find people enjoy it, so maybe I'm a character, too.

Love,
Grandpa

Bombing Tokyo

To Ryan:

Have you seen the television shots of Laguna, California? Since they've been on the last few days, we've seen them time and time again. Every time, they remind me of our firebomb raids on Tokyo. About two hundred to three hundred planes, flying at ten thousand– to fifteen thousand– foot altitudes, dropping incendiary bombs at night. The first night bombing run was to Tokyo. We "hit" the IP (initial point), which was Mount Fujiyama, and turned toward the big city. A "pathfinder" B-29 had already come in earlier and laid down a path of firebombs right through the heart of Tokyo. As we headed in, the first pilot, Capt. Rodenhouse, suggested we "hit" the suburbs to avoid flak, searchlights, and turbulence. The younger crew members, the bombardier, and the copilot—me—said, "No way, we came here to fight a war and we're going down the middle!" He reluctantly agreed. The bombardier took over with his bomb sight and we dumped on target! Capt. Rodenhouse was married with two kids. That night I realized why wars are fought with teenagers and young unmarried men.

Love,
Grandpa

Stay in College

To Ryan:

As I've told you before, Uncle Rob worked at the same company I did for a summer job. The president of the company had a son who worked there, too. It was great experience for both of them. Both were studying to be mechanical engineers. They studied during the school year and worked in the plant during the summers. The wages were good. They received union wages. That was good money for college students, in those days. Most of the other workers in the assembly department where they worked were older men and women. Some were older than I was. One night, as Uncle Rob and I were driving home together, he asked about the pay the other workers got. He thought he knew. When I confirmed that they all received the same as he did, he said, "Well, I'm certainly going to graduate from college. Some assemblers worked there twenty years and get no more than me."

Love,
Grandpa

WEDNESDAY, NOVEMBER 17, 1993

Higgins Philosophy

To Ryan:

You are the first of the next generation in the Higgins family. You have the dubious honor, or maybe misfortune, of being the oldest of our grandchildren. Already you are being subjected to my philosophies. Your mom and your uncles and aunt heard them so often that they devised a system relative to hearing them. Apparently, many of my anecdotes were repeated. I thought it worked for emphasis or touching on a new scenario, but they chalked it up to my having forgotten having told it before! At any rate, when I'd start off on a then-familiar story, they'd all chime in and say, "Well, here comes number six or eight or sixteen or whatever." Well, at least they had the philosophies all committed to memory, and that's what I was really aiming for anyway. I'm logging my notes to you so I don't repeat.

Love you, repeat, love you!

Grandpa

Thanksgiving Tradition

To Ryan:

Happy Thanksgiving Day! While we as Americans celebrate this strictly American custom, it is a singular day. I really do thank God every day for all the good things that we as a family, and I as an individual, benefit from and enjoy living each day. I've felt so strongly about giving thanks that I had our family start a tradition on Thanksgiving. Perhaps your mom told you about it. There's your old grandpa that's different again. At Thanksgiving dinnertime, we'd all relate and share something with the rest of the family about what we were each thankful for. When your Uncle Charlie came up with the comment, "I'm thankful for the same things that Rob just said," I changed the rules. After that, we'd all write down a short note to read at the table of our own thoughts of Thanksgiving. Think about it. Try it. Enjoy. I suggested it last year, too, didn't I?

Love,
Grandpa

WEDNESDAY, DECEMBER 1, 1993

Showing Love

To Ryan:

Your great grandfather, Edward F. Higgins, was a very enthusiastic man. He bragged about his sons and grandchildren a lot. 'Course, we do the same thing. It must come with the territory! Everyone lives in the lives of their offspring. We love you all so much. How does one show their love? I guess that it is in striving to be the best possible in everything we do and say. It's difficult for a lot of people to show the love they have for others. Most of us are embarrassed to demonstrate our love with outward signs. It's especially difficult for young people. It was for me. My dad taught me a good lesson. He had enough self-confidence to kiss his sons out of love. It wasn't—and isn't—unmanly. So I do it now—brother, sons, sons-in-law, grandsons, and, someday, great-grandsons. Think about it.

Love,
Grandpa

St. Anthony Helps Again

To Ryan:

It's almost unbelievable! This morning, after our walk on the beach, it was time to put my contact lenses in my eyes. The bathroom light down here in Florida isn't as good as it is back home in Independence. I've had some problems the last few days "finding" a lens while I was cleaning it in the palm of my hand. As you might imagine, this morning, I lost my left lens. I had dried and wiped my palm between cleansings. It was gone! The towel, the sink, the basin, and my hands, palms, and fingers were all examined in detail. I gave up. Finally, I asked St. Anthony to help find it. I searched again. Grandma came and helped search, too. No success. At last, I called Dr. Weir in Independence to order a replacement lens. Then, I prayed to St. Anthony again, saying, "I haven't given up hope, St. Anthony, please help us find it." Not two minutes later, Grandma found it downstairs on the floor.

Love,

Grandpa

WEDNESDAY, DECEMBER 15, 1993

Body Language

To Ryan:

Wow! Congratulations on your district wrestling award! Your great preparation and fundamentals, coupled with your speed and strength, were awarded again. Good job. You've heard of body language, I'm sure. You know, the messages you send with your body positioning of arms, legs, and torso. Come to think of it, your body language before a wrestling match tells your opponent that he is going to have some kind of match! I've got a new one though. It's "body talk." Over the years, my body "talks" to me. It has said, "Don't ever drink that much again; you'll end up with too much of a headache the morning after." It has said, "Don't eat so much or so fast; you'll get sick and throw up." It has said, "You can do more than that; go for it," or, "Don't over-extend yourself; there's always tomorrow." I listen, and have had a better life because of it. Some people never listen to their body "talk." Do you? Think about it.

Love,
Grandpa

Rob Outing Santa

To Ryan:

Merry Christmas to you and to Brandon, your mom, and Joe! We won't have a "white" Christmas here; hope that you all have one. Hope, too, that Santa is good to you this year! Have you been a good boy? I've been pretty good, so I'm hoping for the best. We got your mom's package today—all gold wrapping, too. Uncle Rob is with us this week and it reminds me of a story. Years ago, after Christmas, Uncle Rob came to us and said, "There is no Santa Claus, you are Santa Claus!" We asked, "What gave you that idea?" He brought out a catalog from John Plain Co., Chicago. He said that he noticed that all the pages with turned-down corners had circled items on the page. Further, all the circled items were presents that your mom, Uncle Charlie, and he had gotten. Smart, eh? Don't tell Brandon. We love you.

Love,
Grandpa

DATE Wednesday 01/19/94

To: Ryan —

MEMORANDUM

... you been watch... the Pro Football ... the ... fans.' Course, ... the playoffs

---

DATE Wednesday 12/07/94

To: Ryan —

MEMORANDUM

Pearl Harbor Day. People living at that time who are still alive, can remember exactly what they were doing that day. I do. About five o'clock that afternoon I was returning home after a pick up football ...

DATE Wednesday 11/02/94

MEMORANDUM

... these football game and your season ... is it worth it, isn't it? You've

DATE Wednesday 04/06/94

MEMO...

DATE Wednesday 02/23/94

To: Ryan —

MEMORANDUM

At times during my career the comp... was working for would have the me... talk to a psychologist. It was a great ... would get an objective look-see at o... One was a particular session that I ... forgotten. He said, "you talk too m... He proceeded to tell me how to over... In a meeting or gathering of peo... If you want to say something, a... about what you want to say, an... to say it, then think about have... ... in the conversation y...

DATE Wednesday 02/02/94

To: Ryan —

MEMORANDUM

We talked about competition and enthusi... last week. Well, wouldn't you know, I... racquetball league I demonstrated that I... was in the third game of the set. I had w... the first game. He had won the second I... was ahead 9 - 6 in the third game. He se... a shot down the left wall. As I went f... the backed into me, and unintentionally ...

1994

WEDNESDAY, JANUARY 5, 1994

New Year's Resolutions

To Ryan:

Happy New Year! I did remember to put '94 on the date above. Often I forget and, due to habit, put down '93. They say that time passes quickly, more so as you get older. I don't find that to be particularly true. I can't wait till Wednesday comes, and we can have our little "chat." I do enjoy every day. I thank God for all He has given to our family and me. My list of New Year's resolutions isn't very long this year. How's yours? It's fun to look back, compare the year before, and see how you did on your New Year's resolutions. I put mine down on a little card and keep it. It reminds me during the year of the things that I wanted to do for others and myself. Then, at the end of the year, I have it to total up my "score." So it's my jumping off spot to start my new list. Some improvements drop off the list. Others I haven't yet "committed to habit," so they go on again. I address some new ones to make me a better me and to help family and others. Enjoy '94. Make it a good year.

Love,
Grandpa

Christmas as a Boy

To Ryan:

I'm still thinking about Christmas. We had many traditions when I was a boy. The very first time I remember Christmas, I remember our tree was on the second floor porch on Thirty-Seventh Street. We were awaiting Santa. I had to go to bed just after dinner to rest, in anticipation of Santa's coming. My folks got me up about 8:00 p.m. We celebrated, opening our gifts. Mom always wrapped everything in white tissue paper with wide paper ribbon. She had had a gift shop years before, and this was all leftover inventory. Then we went to midnight mass. Grandma and I still carry on the Christmas Eve dinner tradition. Her egg crepes with butter and sugar are out of this world. We did it again this year but with ham. It used to be, we didn't eat meat on Christmas Eve. Was your Christmas memorable?

Love,
Grandpa

WEDNESDAY, JANUARY 19, 1994

Enthusiasm in Sports

To Ryan:

Have you been watching the pro football playoffs? We're really Kansas City Chief fans. 'Course, we've watched all the other teams in the playoffs, too. What do you think of the gymnastics or histrionics of those players after they score a touchdown? I mean, I'm all for enthusiasm when you're playing a sport. As a matter of fact, I like to think that I do well in getting my teammates excited, anxious, and all pepped up to extend themselves and do their best on every play, in every game, in order to win. You can get your "juices" flowing. You can get that little extra edge over your opponents whether it's one person, two, four, nine, or eleven. Enthusiasm and competition are two keys in my personality. I think that you've inherited those two, too. Just watch your mom in a Trivial Pursuit game or any other game. All we Higginses (including grandchildren with the last names of Pearce, Genthe, and Barry) are in that category. But watch Marcus Allen after a touchdown. He's a class act. Think about it.

Love,
Grandpa

Playing in the Snow

To Ryan:

Tremendous! Of course I'm enthused! Who wouldn't be after seeing you come from one point down in the second period to win? Great! Congrats! Wrestling potential plus! It was great being with you while there for Aunt Margaret's funeral. However, it was also good to get away from the cold and snow in Milwaukee. There was a time, when I was about Brandon's age or younger, I loved the snow. My Grandma Achtenhagen and I would enjoy it together at home at 1522 South Thirty-Seventh Street. Grandma would go outside and load a tin pan full of snow. She'd bring it into the kitchen sink, and we'd make a small snowman with a pair of raisin eyes and a carrot nose. It had raisin buttons down the front. It took so little to please me and make me happy. It still does. I really enjoy life and all God has given us.

Love,
Grandpa

WEDNESDAY, FEBRUARY 2, 1994

Competition and Enthusiasm

To Ryan:

We talked about competition and enthusiasm last week. Well, wouldn't you know? In my racquetball league I demonstrated that. It was in the third game of the set. I had won the first game. He had won the second. I was ahead nine to six in the third game of the set. He sent a shot down the left wall. As I went after it, he backed into me, unintentionally tripping me. I was really in hot pursuit, so I went sprawling—my head against the wall, my knee to the floor along with my elbow, my thumb and wrist jammed. Probably scared my opponent. He thought I had a concussion, or at least some broken bones in my leg, arm, or wrist. I insisted that we continue the game. I won fifteen to twelve. As a precaution, I went to the doctor the next day. A sprained wrist is all. This Friday, I play in the Senior Olympics Racquetball.

Love,
Grandpa

Striving to Learn from Life

To Ryan:

Well, Senior Olympics Racquetball Tournament is over. Won one, lost two, but had fun, and there's always next year, when I go into the seventy-to-seventy-five age group. Meantime, I'm playing in the racquetball league every week and get in a golf game or two, too. Squeeze in a poker game every Monday, and Rotary meeting every Wednesday. You can see that retirement doesn't mean idleness. As a matter of fact, I can't get all the things done now that I want to do or that Grandma wants me to do. That all seems like a piece of cake for you with your busy schedule, doesn't it? That's good. Get into as many learning experiences as you can. Do the best you are capable of and continually strive to improve by way of what you learn from teachers, family, and friends. Isn't that really what has happened in your wrestling career thus far? The same goes for your academic studies. And your social and life skills. Think about it!

Love,
Grandpa

WEDNESDAY, FEBRUARY 16, 1994

Random Acts of Kindness

To Ryan:

Happy Valentine's Day again! We were so sorry that you and Brandon won't be able to come down to Florida for a couple of days. Maybe next year! So many tourists and "snow birds" around here. Everyone has a camera. Over the years I've developed a habit. I guess it started when we all went to Europe in 1965. Grandma, Uncle Rob, your mom, and Uncle Charlie are in all our pictures of that trip; I took all the pics. So I decided that, whenever I see anyone taking pictures, I offer to take it, so the photographer can be in the snapshot. People are amazed and appreciative of the offer of kindness. Then, recently, I read and heard about the campaign of "Random Acts of Kindness" (RAK) without expectations of return or reward. It's really fun to do something unexpected for someone else, even for strangers. It gives great inner satisfaction. Try to do something nice for family, friends, classmates, and teachers. Think about it.

Love,

Grandpa

Favorites

To Ryan:

What are your favorites? Number? Color? Song? Book? Grandma and I were talking with Aunt Barb and Uncle Mike today about that. I related the story about our being in Monaco at the gambling casino. My mom and dad and Grandma Loe were playing the slot machines. I was at the roulette table. After I had placed and lost all the bets we'd promised for our friends in Zanesville, Ohio, I bet for ourselves. I went to Grandma and asked her favorite number. She thought and said "four," for our four children. I put a dollar chip on four. The croupier spun the wheel and ran the ball. It stopped on four! Wow! I tossed the croupier a dollar from the thirty-five winnings, and walked away. We beat the bank at Monte Carlo! Incidentally, Uncle Rob, Uncle Charlie, and your mom were babysitting themselves that night. Our favorite number is still four. My color is yellow or gold; Grandma's is red. What are your favorites? Think about it.

Love,

Grandpa

WEDNESDAY, MARCH 16, 1994

Premonitions

To Ryan:

Happy St. Patrick's Day! What a memorable experience we had last Friday. Grandma and Aunt Karen are great fans of Perry Como, the singer. So we decided on a day trip to Jupiter, Florida, his hometown. After a two- to three-hour leisurely trip down there, Charlie had a premonition to stop to ask directions. Following the directions from the gas station, we proceeded to Jupiter Island. After I made a directed turn, Charlie suggested a return turn into a guarded development. We were still on a search for Perry's house. Charlie decided to ask two old gents walking the road ahead. We stopped. To answer Charlie's inquiry about Perry's house location, the nearest man said, "You've got to be kidding!" He looked us all over carefully. Then he turned to the other man and said, "They're looking for Perry Como's house!" You guessed it. Perry Como walked over to our car! We've got pictures of all of us with Perry. Aunt Karen has his autograph, too. Premonition works. Think about it.

Love,
Grandpa

"Type A" Personalities

To Ryan:

While walking the beach the other day, we met a fisherman. Grandma remarked that I would never make a good fisherman. I had just noticed that the fellow was very efficient. He had gutted and beheaded his catch thus far while waiting for another bite. Grandma said that's what I would do—look for a shortcut, a change, or a better way of doing things. I would never be content to sit still and just fish. Grandma was kidding me about being an "A" type personality, anxious and impatient. Thinking about it, I guess that she is right. On the other hand, maybe it isn't so bad to be looking for improvements and to be positive in searching for efficiency—if one doesn't do it to a fault. Think about it.

Love,
Grandpa

The Mark of a Class Act

To Ryan:

Did you have Palmer penmanship and writing classes in grade school? Does Brandon have such classes now? Probably neither of you did. I did. I hope that it shows. That is, I hope that anyone can read my writing. Sometimes I print, just so my words and messages can be read better than my writing. Just for fun, next time all the Higgins clan is together, ask for everyone's autograph. Not before, but after they all sign, check the signatures. Which would a stranger be able to read? From my experience, women generally have very legible, readable penmanship. Men don't. Just like a firm handshake, a smile, and looking the other person straight in the eye, I think writing and penmanship, particularly one's own readable autograph or signature, is a mark of a class act.

Love,
Grandpa

Higgins Savings & Loan

To Ryan:

Income tax day! April 15 each year we get to help support our form of government by paying taxes. Fortunately, we have money to pay. The government anticipates that some people don't or won't budget to pay at the proper time—April 15 each year. They insist that everyone pays monthly through their company, or every three months through direct, estimated tax payments to the IRS. Have you ever tried budgeting? You've twenty-four hours a day to spend. If you don't budget, formally or informally, you still expend all that time. You're so busy, I expect that you would like more hours in your day. How about money? Do you have enough in your control to be able to budget? Have your mom tell you about the "Higgins Savings & Loan Association." We ran our own banking within the family. I kept the books. Uncle Rob, Uncle Charlie, Aunt Barb, and your mom deposited their allowances and earned money using their "Higgins bank books." They wrote checks on their accounts when they wanted to spend some of their money. Think you can budget spending? Try. Think about it.

Love,
Grandpa

Flowers in Window Boxes

To Ryan:

Grandma and I went spring shopping this week. That's getting in a whole bunch of geraniums for our window boxes. We only get red ones because that's Grandma's favorite color. The custom goes way back to the time that the family went to Europe. Your mom and Uncle Rob were exchange students in Germany. My parents, Uncle Charlie, Grandma, and I went over to pick them up in August of 1965. Part of our touring trip was through Switzerland. It seemed as though all the houses and chalets had beautiful flowers blooming in their window boxes. Many of the farmhouses were built above the stable below. But everyone had flowers. When we got home, and ever since, I have built window boxes wherever we have lived. I think your mom and Aunt Barb inherited Grandma's and my "green thumb." We used to grow vegetables, too; however, Grandma says I like to plant, but that I don't like to weed.

Love,
Grandpa

Memories of War

To Ryan:

We talked to a workman this week, ending up in a war discussion. You get veterans together, and soon they will be reliving the war they were in. I remember a bombing raid over Tokyo. We had laid down incendiary bombs. Naturally, after the bomb run, we were anxious to get out of there as fast as we could go. It was past midnight. We had no "running" lights on for fear of detection by enemy fighters. They generally used antiaircraft "flak" against us on the way into the target and fighters after. All of a sudden, the tail gunner reported a "ball of fire" on our tail. The "ball of fire" was a jet kamikaze fighter—the jet exhaust responsible for the so-called "ball of fire" visible in the night sky. Just as I was about to give the order to the gunmen to open fire, the tail gunner reported tracer bullets going toward the fighter from another B-29. The gunners all watched as the distance from tracer origination, the B-29, to the target, the ball of fire, got shorter. Finally, there was a huge explosion as the B-29 was rammed by the Japanese fighter. It lit up the whole night sky. Three large pieces of flaming debris floated down into Tokyo Bay below. It turned out to be that the pilot was a good buddy of mine.

Love,
Grandpa

WEDNESDAY, MAY 4, 1994

Getting Certified in CPR

To Ryan:

What would you do if someone in the school cafeteria started choking? Think about it. One of my New Year's Resolutions was to learn and be certified in first aid and CPR. I'd had some training in years past. Times change. New methods and techniques evolve in about everything that we do at home, school, and work. So I signed up. Last week I took instruction from the American Red Cross. Today I am again certified in first aid for three years and CPR for one year. I feel pretty confident now that I can assist in any emergency that I encounter. It must give great joy and personal satisfaction for a person to save someone's life, or at least help in doing so. At your age, I learned my first aid in the Boy Scout program. Do they teach any of that in school these days? Take an hour or so and page through a first aid book. It might help someone.

Love,
Grandpa

Don't Be a Squirrel

To Ryan:

Are you a squirrel? Figuratively, that is. I tend to be one . . . and Grandma agrees. I hate to throw anything away. I figure that I maybe can use it someday. If not me, then someone else will be able to use it to his or her comfort or advantage. I should know better. Years ago I took over a manager's job as the quality control manager. Coming in fresh, I went through my predecessor's files and threw out a lot. He was a good friend who was retiring. I wondered how he justified keeping all those files, letters, and records. Six months later, I found that my file drawers were bulging. I had fallen into the same trap. After reorganizing, I devised a system to keep only essential files. Even so, periodically, a review of files, tools, clothing, and equipment is necessary. Do you use all the stuff you have in drawers, closets, and shelves? Think about it. Don't be a squirrel.

Love,
Grandpa

WEDNESDAY, MAY 25, 1994

Being a "Toucher"

To Ryan:

Everyone has his or her own set of characteristics. Some are good, some are not so good. In total, they determine each person's personality and reputation. Sometimes it's body movements (some call it "body language") that "speak" for a person. In order to develop your perception of people, a person should know and study some of those characteristics. Here's one that you can watch for, Ryan. I am a "toucher"! As I talk to others, invariably I will reach out and touch the other person. It may be a hand on the shoulder, or on the forearm, or touching hand to hand. For me, it is an expression of friendliness, and, with family, love for the other person. It's interesting that many people who are "touchers" don't realize it until they are told. What do you think? Is it a good characteristic? Are you a toucher? Most young people aren't. Some use it to get attention or to emphasize a point. Think about it.

Love,
Grandpa

Choosing a Career

To Ryan:

When I graduated from high school, I knew that I wanted to go to college. My idea was to follow my brothers, Ed and Chuck, into the engineering field. When I graduated from college as a mechanical engineer, I was undecided as to whether to go into sales engineering, manufacturing, or development engineering. I was prepared for starting out in any of those three major divisions. Cornell University did that. So, during my senior year, I had contacted and visited six different companies who had Cornell engineers as top executives: two in sales, two in manufacturing, and two in developmental engineering. I asked each one of them to help me decide which division to pursue. You'd think each would recommend his own specialty. But here is what they said: all of them said selling oneself was the key. In sales, you sold yourself, and then your product. In manufacturing, you sold yourself and then company techniques. And in development, you sold yourself and then your designs. I think that you are a salesman. Do you?

Love,
Grandpa

WEDNESDAY, JUNE 8, 1994

Doing Random Acts of Kindness

To Ryan:

Have you had many RAKs lately? You know . . . Random Acts of Kindness! It's become somewhat of a game for Grandma and me. We see each other doing something for another person, and we slip each other a "Nice RAK you just did!" Try it. It needn't be any big deal. Some of mine lately: gave a lil' ole lady the extra pennies she needed to pay her bill instead of searching in her purse, helped an old gent run his work on a five-cent copy machine in the store, and directed a couple who were obviously lost toward their intended destination. Seems as though we all have forgotten to do those lil' helpful things for others. I get great satisfaction from doing things like that. 'Course, I guess I get pretty forward sometimes, offering to help out of a clear blue sky. It's worth it, though, seeing the surprise, appreciation, or delight in people's faces when I do it. Try it. It will make you a better you.

Love,
Grandpa

Following Leaders' Orders

To Ryan:

It goes way back in my working life, but let me share one of my experiences that really taught me a lot. The essence of it was, "Don't be two jerks if you only have to be one," or, "Don't get people upset twice when it need be only once." A shop foreman worked for me. When an edict (order) came out from "higher-ups," he would change its enforcement for his employees in the mistaken belief that he was showing them what a nice guy he was. Then later, top management would hear of it and insist that he follow orders as originally handed down. He was a jerk to management. When he went back to his people and enforced the order as originally given, they all said, "What a jerk." He was despised twice, by those above and below. Instead, if he'd have followed orders originally, maybe his people would have badmouthed him as a jerk. But really, they probably would realize he was only following orders. Lesson: follow your leader and orders so that someday you can be the leader and give orders.

Love,
Grandpa

WEDNESDAY, JUNE 22, 1994

New Adventures in Montana

To Ryan:

You are a busy young man this summer with your camps. Your mom told us about your latest and all that you're learning about wrestling techniques. That's great. Good luck! I should say, keep up the good work. A person pretty well makes their own so-called "luck" by hard work, persistence, learning experiences, and studies. Now that you're one fourth of your way through your high school studies, are you having fun? Your grades are showing that you are learning and progressing. Now what about your new adventure in Montana? You must be excited. New school system, new friends, new neighbors, new teachers, new town, new beautiful home and countryside . . . and, to help you enjoy all these new experiences, you have your loving family. Stay in there, hit the books, study hard, look 'em straight in the eye, give a firm handshake, speak up forcefully, and maybe even take that debate course or join the debate team next year. You have a great smile, so smile. Think about it.

Love,
Grandpa

Patriotism and Family

To Ryan:

Would you be willing to risk your life for your country? These days a lot of people are saying that patriotism is lacking in the United States. Patriotism isn't just waving a flag or mouthing a lot about love of country. One thing about democracy, though, is that a person can say or act just about any way they want. But if a non-American were to badmouth the good ole USA, watch out. You'd hear and see citizens come to the defense—actually, Americans would probably go to the offense instead. 'Course, families follow a similar path: debate among family members but a solid front against all non-family. Back to patriotism—Fourth of July weekend! I get duck-bumps seeing the flag in a parade. I get a catch in my throat singing the National Anthem. And, yes, I risked my life during World War II for the United States. Be proud! Be happy to be an American. Think about it.

Love,
Grandpa

WEDNESDAY, JULY 20, 1994

Family Trips

To Ryan:

Suggestion: You all are going on many trips as a family, so you might be interested in some experiences your mom and the rest of us had on our trips. For years, whenever we'd stop at "tourist traps," gas stations, and restaurants, Uncle Rob, your mom, Uncle Charlie, and Aunt Barb would always look for souvenirs. As they grew older, we devised a plan to avoid confrontations, arguments, and unhappiness. At the start of a long trip, we'd appoint a family treasurer. Uncle Rob, being oldest, was the first in line. He'd get a twenty- or fifty-dollar kitty to start. All payments went to Uncle Rob's control. Gas, food, and souvenirs were all paid for by Uncle Rob, or whoever was the "treasurer" of the day. You'd be amazed at the control exercised. Great training in spending, budgeting, and conservation of capital. Ask your mom to be "treasurer of the trip."

Love,
Grandpa

Coded Messages

To Ryan:

During our trip to Milwaukee, it was just great being with you again. Too bad it couldn't have been longer. I was reminded of some of my "coded messages." When your mom was a girl, she and Uncle Rob, Uncle Charlie, and Aunt Barb caused me to devise a code in order to avoid embarrassing them. As the occasion demanded, I would say "GRRR." That was to represent the GR, which in turn was for the "Golden Rule": to treat others as you would have others treat you! If they heard me "GRRR," they knew that I thought they weren't being very nice to someone, so shape up! Another "code" was "CAT": be sure that you are Communicating as you should, make certain that you have the right Attitude, and know that Timing is of the essence. You can have one or two of the above, but mess up the third, and lose your effectiveness. Think about it! GR or CAT.

Love,
Grandpa

Cut and Choose

To Ryan:

Tomorrow is your birthday! Happy birthday, big fifteen-year-old! At least we had a little time with you in Milwaukee. Maybe we can get up to Montana and you can show us around your new "digs." In the meantime, we hope to get to sing "Happy Birthday to You" tomorrow, at your dad's house. We love you! Following last week's letter relative to family traditions, hear this . . . Apropos of your birthday, whenever we had birthday cakes or other treats, we would have a "cut and choose" technique. We had to start it to get over all the arguments about who was to get which piece of cake, watermelon, pie, or candy. Then (and now) one person divides the dessert, and the others get to choose what piece to take. You can see that the divider will take great care to ensure that the division is as equal as possible. Try that technique with your buddies. It works. Think about it.

Love,

Grandpa

Reputation and Impressions

To Ryan:

Some time back I became aware of an expression that kind of shook me up a bit. It was: "Always remember that your name will travel a lot farther than your face ever will." The key to the encouragement and understanding of that phrase is *reputation*. Be sure that you do the right thing, in everything that you do. You might think that no one knows you, but you'd be surprised at how many people will know your name and recognize it . . . for good or bad. That thought, combined with "first impressions," are paramount in your new surroundings in Montana. You keep up that quick smile and friendliness, firm handshake, and neat appearance with your new neighbors, school- and teammates, and teachers— you're a cinch to give a good first impression and start on your way to a good reputation.

Love,
Grandpa

WEDNESDAY, AUGUST 31, 1994

Moving to Shorewood

To Ryan:

During your move to a new home and school, I thought about the time my folks moved from Milwaukee's south side to Shorewood. I was just going into high school, the ninth grade. You'd think that I would have visited my old buddies and neighborhood a lot after the move. I didn't go back but once, even though I didn't know one person in the new neighborhood and school. I wished that school had started right away, but I had the whole summer to try to get to know new friends. Once school did begin, it was a lot easier because there were lots of different classes and sports. I ended up with a good group of friends. The reason? Students gravitate toward others that think the same way as they do. I did my best to do well in class and made good grades. I took up playing the saxophone. I went out for football end. I had fun. I enjoyed meeting and being with the kind of people I wanted to be with. I know that you can be successful—and will! Try it.

Love,
Grandpa

Mother Knows Best

To Ryan:

Aunt Barb, Sam, and Brian are visiting us. An incident of "mother knows best" reminded me of the time I finally acknowledged that axiom. My mom had come up to West Point for my graduation as an Army Air Force pilot. As part of the occasion, all the graduates had ordered new dress uniforms, including a hat with a bill, military style. Mine was wool, and mighty smooth and flawless. After the ceremony, Mom and I went to New York City for dinner and a show. Afterward we came out of a restaurant. It was raining. We were under a canopy, so it wasn't raining on us yet, but cabs were hard to get due to the crowds. I was so worried about getting my new hat wet. Mom insisted that it wouldn't harm it, but I still held back. Finally, in desperation, I ran out and got a cab for us, even though I got wet. The next day my hat was great. Mother knew best! A little incident, but I learned. Think about it.

Love,
Grandpa

WEDNESDAY, SEPTEMBER 21, 1994

Teenage Drivers

To Ryan:

I'm enclosing a newspaper article regarding teenage drivers. Your mom and I talked about your approaching the age when you will be getting your driver's license. I'll bet that you are really anxious. I was. I'm reminded of another young man, just as anxious. He studied cars from the time he was old enough to recognize the differences among makes and models. He could quote performance details about the most popular ones. He was a good kid—not a wise guy, a show off, or a dummy. So, when he reached the age of sixteen, he easily passed both the written and driving tests. Since his folks could afford it, they gave him a nice car for his sixteenth birthday. They had tried not to spoil him growing up. He was an adopted child—their only child. They had succeeded. He was a bright, articulate, mechanically-minded lad. The night of his sixteenth birthday he took his car for a ride, alone. He wrapped it around a tree, killing him. Think about it.

Love,
Grandpa

The Challenges of Driving

To Ryan:

I've turned over a new leaf in my driving. Earlier this year, in Florida, Uncle Charlie kidded me about my driving. That did it! Grandma has for years said that I drive too fast and make passengers uncomfortable. I resolved to henceforth drive no faster than the speed limit. Formerly, I'd allow myself up to five miles per hour over. It's amazing—now everyone complains that I drive too slowly. I feel great, although I do allow a plus or minus one-mile-per-hour variation. Also, Grandma comments about my swivel neck—I look around too much. That comes from being a pilot. I was trained to be on the lookout for other planes (and UFOs!) from all directions. I can't get out of that habit. I do look right, left, front, and behind constantly. I call that driving defensively. It pays to look out for less cautious drivers. Had any RAKs lately? The other day, after finishing copying something, a couple of old folks wanted to use the machine. I helped. Try it.

Love,
Grandpa

Success vs. Achievement

To Ryan:

Some time ago, Uncle Rob was questioning his company's philosophy on success. It had to do with being ruthless in order to be successful. He said, "Dad, you're not ruthless; how come you're successful?" My reply: "Uncle Rob, some people may indeed think that I'm ruthless, though I don't think that I am. I try to call my decisions honestly, in line with my company's policies, fairly, and with sensitivity to the person and occasion. If I am successful, it's because I go 'one step' beyond that which is required of me by my company, family, associates—whomever or whatever the occasion." Incidentally, know the difference between success and achievement! Achievement is the knowledge that you have studied, worked hard, and done the best that's in you. Success is being praised by others. That's nice, but not as important or satisfying. Always aim for achievement.

Love,
Grandpa

Wishes

To Ryan:

How many times have you heard someone say, "Isn't that great? I wish that I could do that." Let me share with you some of my wishes. I like music. I wish that I could sit down and play the piano . . . by ear, that is, without having to read the music. My Uncle Joe Higgins could do that. It's a God-given talent—but if I had followed my parents' advice and suggestions, I'd have taken piano lessons at a young age. Then, today I could have sat down and played. I did learn to play the saxophone for four years in high school. So I really understand and appreciate music. Same with debate. I wish I had taken debate in high school—although I don't know if they taught it at my school. I did overcome shyness—forced myself to talk and question people. Now I'm not afraid of speaking to a big crowd. Think about it. Wish!

Love,
Grandpa

WEDNESDAY, OCTOBER 19, 1994

Rotary

To Ryan:

Rotary is an organization made up of the top woman or man in each company or profession in town. Its motto is "Service Above Self." The members are to consider this four-way test in everything that they do—in their family, work, and community. Is it the truth? Is it fair to all concerned? Will it build goodwill and better friendships? Will it be beneficial to all concerned? That's all pretty simple and easy to understand, isn't it? It's almost like a Ten Commandments for Business. I guess that it could apply to students, too. Not that I'm proposing that, mind you. It's just something to think about . . . service above self. That's pretty altruistic, but, as Grandma always says, "When you give of yourself, you will get much in return." That all sounds like it ties in with RAK (random acts of kindness). How many RAKs have you had lately?

Love,
Grandpa

Election Day Judging

To Ryan:

Yesterday was Election Day. I voted, as did Grandma. However, I spent the whole day as a judge at one of the polling spots. That is, they had three Democrats and three Republicans monitoring the voting at our location. I was one of the Republican judges. What an experience that was! About 51 percent of the eligible voters in our precinct cast a ballot. It felt good to be part of the democratic process of electing officials for our government. Make sure that you register to vote as soon as you are twenty-one. It is a privilege that many other people in the world wish that they had. It is a responsibility for every citizen. Whenever I hear anyone complain about an official, I ask, "Did you vote?" You have no right to complain if you weren't part of the process of voting.

Love,
Grandpa

Avoiding Profanity

To Ryan:

What do you say if you accidentally hit your thumb with the hammer? If I do that, or have some other traumatic experience, I say, "Sacre blue put cimmoni toni, yuap she daubnutz!" That's a phonetic translation. I really don't know what it means, or if it is in any modern language. I copied it from my brother Ed. However, it does give vent to my immediate emotions. Yet it doesn't offend anyone. Your mom and our other kids have all heard it innumerable times. You know, I never heard my father swear, blaspheme, or use vulgar language. I don't think that our children ever heard me say anything other than the above quotation. I adapted my "sacre blue, etc.," to avoid profanity. Think up one. Try it; make it meaningless and demonstrative, but not profane. Think about it.

Love,
Grandpa

Playing "Pretend"

To Ryan:

Happy Thanksgiving! We'd sing if we were together, you know, "Happy Thanksgiving" to the tune of "Happy Birthday." You're probably in a better position than you have been to play "pretend." Grandma and I, with four other friends, were out in western Colorado a few years back. We were just driving and enjoying the scenic view, when I said, "Let's play pretend." I suggested that we consider how it would have been in pioneer times out near the Rocky Mountains in a covered wagon. Everyone "jumped in" with the ideas. One said, "I'll be the point man while you all prepare to circle the wagons." One lady said, "I'll get the fires going and prepare the food to cook our evening meal. It will be buffalo steaks, hard pone, and coffee." Another said, "I'll take my gun and hunt for some game for tomorrow." We mentally eliminated the telephone poles and scattered houses. It was interesting fun. Out in Montana, outside of town, ought to be great pretend territory. Think about it. Happy Thanksgiving again.

Love,
Grandpa

WEDNESDAY, NOVEMBER 30, 1994

Reading Instructions

To Ryan:

Congratulations on your first deer! You know that in all the years I have hunted, I never did get my own deer. I followed all the instructions, but no luck. How many times have you heard the expression, "When all else fails, read the instructions?" In your career, you'll run across instances many times when you will be asked to follow instructions; you've probably already had that scenario many times. Reminds me of one time in college, we were given instructions to read prior to a test. The time limit on the test was very short. That caused many of us to hurry. Some failed to read the instructions, cause they started off with the usual; that is, "Be sure to read the instructions, all of them, before starting the test," "read all questions before answering," "complete each, answering before going on to the next one," etc. The last instruction was, "Do not answer any question. Hand in your paper now, the test is over!"

Love,

Grandpa

Pearl Harbor

To Ryan:

Pearl Harbor Day! People living at that time who are still alive can remember exactly what they were doing that day. I do. About five o'clock that afternoon, I was returning home after a pick-up football game. Our dog, Pepper, was outside. He ran across the field to greet me. As I entered the house, my folks told me about Pearl Harbor. It completely changed my life. I was just a tad older than you are now—in high school, enjoying life. Seven months later, I graduated from high school. Seven months after that, I was in the Army Air Force. I had completed one semester at Cornell. I was anxious to go. I was patriotic, enthusiastic, full of vim and vigor, and ready to fight for our country, go places, do things, and come back to family, friends, and college afterward.

Love,
Grandpa

Thinking Confidently

To Ryan:

It was great talking to you. Good to hear about your hunting prowess. Wish that mine was as good. Your hunting success reminds me of this quote that I read just yesterday: "If you think that you can or if you think that you can't, you're probably right." Think about it. 'Course, it means that if you think you're going to lose, you probably will end up losing. On the other hand, most winners are extremely self-confident, and think that they are going to win. That doesn't mean that they are cocky or braggadocios. Matter of fact, while confident and thinking that they are going to succeed, all I've talked to, including myself, are nervous before getting into the scene. Think about "you can."

Love,
Grandpa

Childhood Christmas Traditions

To Ryan:

It must be the season for memories. When I sit back and gaze at our Christmas tree, I reminisce about family traditions and memorable events of the past. It was almost ritualistic when I was a boy. We'd have dinner in early evening. It was always egg crepes and milk. Mom would whip up a big batch for Dad, us three boys, and my grandma and Uncle Frank, when they were still alive. No meat on Fridays or Christmas Eve, in those days. Then, when I was very young, I'd go to bed for a short nap, in order for Santa to come and bring the tree and presents. Later, we'd all go to midnight mass. After that, we'd rush home to open presents and eat some cookies and candy. We'd finally go to bed at about three or four in the morning. Hope that you have a merry Christmas!

Love,

Grandpa

New Year's Resolutions

To Ryan:

Happy New Year! Nineteen ninety-four has gone by fast, but the older you get, it seems, the faster they go. Just reviewed this past year's resolutions. I did accomplish all but one. The one I didn't finish was to write one page per week on my garage sale book. I may include that this year. One that I'm sure to include is to become more accomplished on the computer. To that end, I just today enrolled in a computer class at the local high school. I'm thinking about doing some sculpting in paper-mache, maybe even making a big mask or head for parades and parties. Already, I've made a six-foot-tall Nutcracker soldier (two or three years ago), and a five-foot-high heart—red, of course. On one side I wrote, "Loe, I love you—Me" and gave it to Grandma on her birthday, January 31. Then, on the other side I wrote, "Happy Valentine's Day." Both messages were in white paint. Did you know that my dad's birthday is February 14? We put the heart in the yard.

Love,
Grandpa

DATE Wednesday 02/22/95

To: Ryan -

MEMORANDUM

DATE Wednesday 11/01/95

To: Ryan -

MEMORANDUM

There's an old saying that the elderly think mostly
about two things: eating and being "regular." Do
you know what being regular means in that
instance? I guess I first the expression when I
was about your age — well, maybe two years older.
I was about to go into the ar—

DATE Wednesday 04/12/95

MEMORANDUM

every Tuesday at noon I go to Rotary.
nization of the "movers and

DATE Wednesday 02/05/95

MEMORANDUM

DATE Wednesday 07/12/95

To: Ryan -

MEMORANDUM

You've heard of one-ups-manship —
is, when someone tries/does out
another person. It can be in spo
business, family, or the political
Well, I recently heard again the
would you believe, the Golden
person asked if anyone had he
Platinum Rule. Platinum be
precious than gold, I figured t
"... be a better philosophy

DATE Wednesday 06/28/9

To: Ryan -

MEMORANDUM

Do you remember ever seeing me wearing
long straight tie? I was trying to remem
the last time that I did. I think that
wore a bow tie in college for awhile alth
we seldom wore ties there. On the other h
my entire senior year at Cornell I wore long
That was to get used to wearing shirt, ties

1995

WEDNESDAY, JANUARY 4, 1995

Planning for the Future

To Ryan:

So how's everything working out? How's school? Signed up for debate yet? Football is over, but I expect you're still working out on your weight lifting. You probably hang with your jock buddies, but girls don't play football, so now you will have some time to spend on other stuff—like girls, school, classes, extracurricular clubs, band, and planning. Joe and your mom are great in planning for the future. It pays. And you know, you can still have fun in high school while you plan or direct your activities to things that you'll use and get experience in as you get older. I was kind of hoping that you'd spend five dollars of your hard-earned money to get into the investment contest in the Higgins Monthly. You can follow the selections of everyone in the family. I'll bet that Grandma wins. Did you have a good Christmas and New Year's Day? We did. Write down your New Year's resolutions. We did!

Love,
Grandpa

Anticipate, Don't React

To Ryan:

"Anticipate, don't just react!" When I read that the other day, I thought of you. That has to be your credo when you're going to be playing safety on the football team next fall. I always considered that characteristic high on the list when I thought about hiring or promoting anyone that ever worked with me. In turn, I tried to anticipate and then act on it when it came to dealing with my own boss, our customers, competitors, and fellow workers. It's particularly helpful when preparing for negotiations—in my case, especially in union contract negotiations. I guess that it is, in some ways, analogous to "putting yourself in the other person's shoes," to see or feel what they're thinking or how they'll react. Think about it. Anticipate!

Love,
Grandpa

WEDNESDAY, JANUARY 18, 1995

Being a Good Listener

To Ryan:

We've talked about "listening" before. One more lil' story about listening that really convinced me, years ago, about the advantages of being a good listener. In one of the companies where I worked, most of the office staff would go out to eat at a local diner. There I got to observe many of our employees. The president's secretary, a good friend, often ate there with many different people as lunch companions. She was different. No matter with whom she was dining, she never scanned the room, and always appeared to be raptly intent on what the other person was saying. I realized that those were the reasons that everyone liked her and credited her with being such a good conversationalist and good listener. Since then, I've increased my efforts to be a good listener. I hope that I'm gaining on it.

Love,
Grandpa

Public Speaking

To Ryan:

Somewhere down the line, you're going to be speaking to a large audience, Mr. President! You'll be talking about subjects that you know, you'll be enthusiastic, and you'll smile appropriately (like you're doing right now!). You'll build your speech plan, point by point. You'll be speaking slowly and positively, you'll emphasize your main point, and you'll close your short presentation and sit down. All of that before the audience has a chance to get restless, sleepy, bored, or disinterested. Check yourself out. Next time you're talking to someone, notice their reactions. Are they looking past you or away from you? Do they look as though they can't wait till you're finished, or till they can tell their story? These are some ways to judge your own effectiveness in communication. Good speakers can "read" their audiences and listeners. Can you? I'm still learning!

Love,
Grandpa

WEDNESDAY, FEBRUARY 8, 1995

Habits and the Rosary

To Ryan:

Last year or so, we "talked" about habits. You know, like cutting the tip off the pie whenever you start eating it. Also, have you been successful in remembering to put 1995 when you've had to date something lately? A lot of people, through force of habit, are still using 1994. Well, I thought of another habit, developed over the years, and for legitimate good reason. I always put my wallet in my left front pant pocket. I also put my little red Swiss knife there. In my right front pocket, I have my handkerchief. Accompanying it is a blue plastic coin holder. Instead of coins, though, I carry my rosary. Those few things go into my pants every day— besides my two legs, of course. Interestingly, the rosary is sterling silver, given to me by your Grandma Loe when I went overseas during World War II. It flew with me on every mission against Japan, too. Habit, yeah, but it also carried for me thoughts of Grandma and God.

Love,

Grandpa

Word Processor

This was the first letter to be typed instead of handwritten.

To Ryan:

You are the recipient of my first experience on the word processor section of the Microsoft Works program on our PS/1 computer. I have been going to classes every week in order to learn, just to get familiar with the whole process. Then when I started to practice at home on our own computer, I realized that the tutorial lessons on our computer were not only the same as those in class, but that ours were even better than theirs. My very first attempt was on the Higgins Investment Sweepstakes that Uncle Charlie started in his monthly Higgins newsletter, as of the first of the year. Maybe you have peeked at the copy that you all get at Canary Lane? The next issue, coming out this month, will show the results to date as written on this computer. As you will see, both Joe and your mom are on the positive side. Also, yours truly and Uncle Mike, the two supposedly most knowledgeable of the crew, are in the negative end of the scenario.

Continued on next page

Unfortunately, this little note has taken me about twice the time that it would were I to handwrite it out. However, it is great experience. When I get to the point that I don't have to make so many corrections, I'll think about typing your notes on this word processor.

"Speaking" of gambling, this Saturday Mr. Hopper and I are going to be dealers of blackjack at one of the local church's benefit parties. It will get me in shape for the time that Grandma and I go to the riverboat casinos for another try at our luck. About a month or so ago we went with some friends, and it was interesting. I sort of watched, because I really don't like to go gamble with the professionals. I'd rather play cards with friends or family. At least then you know that your losses are going to a good cause! As you can see, I haven't mastered the finite details of getting the date, your name, and the first sentence to come out at the exact spot that I want them to be. On to more practice. They, and I, say—practice makes for perfection.

Love,
Grandpa

New Projects and Success

To Ryan:

So, how did your spaghetti dinner come out? It must have given you a good feeling. When a person attempts a new project and successfully completes it—wow! Let me reminisce: We had just moved into our first apartment, which we had to furnish ourselves. We moved in a big, old, gray mohair couch from the local used furniture store. It was worn; the color was depressing. Grandma was pregnant with Uncle Rob. We agreed that a slipcover was needed for the couch. Because of the cost of getting it done by an upholsterer, I decided to slipcover it myself. My mom had taught me how to use a sewing machine, so we bought a used one. A visit to the library furnished me with detailed instructions on slipcovering, including the cording, heading, and edging. I did it in green. It lasted till we could afford a new one, years later.

Love,
Grandpa

WEDNESDAY, FEBRUARY 29, 1995

Two-Dollar Bills

To Ryan:

Heard you changed from spaghetti to Chinese for your girlfriend. How unusual for a young man to prepare a meal for a friend in his home! Good idea . . . good for you! That's the way I like to do things, too, the unusual-but-good things. I started my two-dollar bill project that way—just to have fun and be different, in a no-one-gets-burned kind of a deal. Sort of a "don't be one of the herd" scenario. The epitome of the two-dollar bill scene was when I'd get a stack of them. The bank would give me a pack of brand new bills. I'd prepare two pieces of cardboard exactly the same size as a two-dollar bill. After putting one on each side of the stack, I'd rubber cement one side of the stack completely, including the cardboard. Then, whenever I paid a restaurant, gas, grocery, or services tab, I'd whip out my pad of bills, flip up the cardboard cover, and proceed to tear off one bill after another, just like a note pad. The cashiers would be flabbergasted. The "rip-off," plus the two-dollar bills, was almost too much for some of them. As a matter of fact, some almost refused to take the money. Some felt they were worth a lot more than two dollars. You found that out when you sold some of yours for three dollars, eh?

Love,

Grandpa

Proper Speech

To Ryan:

Did you catch my error on the date of the last note (February 29, 1995)? I just added seven days to the date of the previous note! Grandma and I were listening to TV recently regarding "manner of speaking." Poorly educated and disadvantaged students were being trained in "business English," versus their "street English." I didn't realize the variation existed to the extent they talked about. When I was growing up, my parents insisted on "Yes, sir," "No, sir," "Yes, ma'am," and "No ma'am," spoken clearly and loudly, along with proper grammar, pronunciation, and good English. It was emphasized to the students that they had to speak well in order to get and keep a good job in society today. So Grandma now insists that I go back to my roots. No more "uh huh"; it's "yes ma'am" again. Then I talked to your mom, and she uses "yeah" incessantly. Help her correct that for me, will you? Think about it.

Love,
Grandpa

Writing to Congress

To Ryan:

How often do you read the newspaper? Our next-door neighbor doesn't get a paper. I think that she, a single mother with a seven-year-old, probably is so busy and possibly feels that she gets enough news à la TV. 'Course, nowadays about all it seems that one hears or reads about is O. J. or Congress. Congressional people have a tough job to do, trying to satisfy all their constituents and still vote the "right" way. Years ago I wrote our Missouri senators on a subject that I was much concerned about. Interestingly, after dictating the letter, my secretary opined that she felt diametrically opposite to my viewpoint. I suggested that she write a similar letter to mine but with the opposite advice, suggestions, and demands. Neither was on company stationery—just ordinary citizens relating to our representatives in Washington. Guess what! Both our replies came back—with identical messages—"Thanks for writing. I'll take your thoughts into my deliberations." Think about it. Try it yourself.

Love,
Grandpa

Don't Criticize Others

To Ryan:

From time to time, in my readings I run across succinct writings and sayings that get right to the "meat" of a subject. Here's one by E. C. Simpson:

> Don't criticize your enemies. It was you who made them.
> Don't criticize your friends. You'll make them enemies.
> Don't criticize people you don't know. You'll make enemies of the people who have to listen to you.
> That leaves nobody for you to criticize but yourself.
> And depending on how you do that, you can be your own friend or your own enemy.

The key to all that is how you approach, judge, and present. I try to use the Golden Rule when I find something or someone who doesn't live up to my expectations. If I could just learn to think a little, before I open my big mouth. Think about it.

Love,
Grandpa

WEDNESDAY, APRIL 12, 1995

Smile

To Ryan:

About every Tuesday at noon, I go to Rotary. It's an organization of the "movers and shakers" in town—owners, presidents, chief executives, general managers, and professionals. We have lunch and a program, sing a bit, and visit with the other "top dogs." It's fun. It's interesting. We try to sing this song every time: "Smile."

> Smile, and the world smiles with you,
> Sing a song,
> Don't be weary, just be cheery all day long.
> Whenever your trials, your troubles, and your cares
> Seem to be more than you can really bear,
> Just smile, and the world smiles with you,
> Sing a song!

Pretty good thoughts there. I know that I don't smile enough. I've even got a little card that reads "Smile" on my desk to remind me. When we get together, I'll sing it to you so you can capture the tune. Do you smile enough? Can't be too much smiling, too much to be thankful for. Think about it.

Love,
Grandpa

How to "Get Over It"

To Ryan:

"Get over it"—I'd not heard that expression before. Someone was writing about a person who was harboring a resentment. His advice was to "get over it," leave it behind, forget it, don't mess up your life carrying a grudge. On thinking about it, it made sense to me. Unless the transgressor truly meant it as an affront, he or she has probably forgotten it, or never realized that it was a hurt. Sometimes it takes the form of braggadocio and "trash talking." In those cases, I use my favorite expression for that kind of person, "Consider the source and ignore it." On the other hand, if the person really did something intentionally to damage you, your reputation, or your family, look for the reasoning behind it, correct things if that's what's called for, repair any damages that you can, go on with your life, and "get over it"!

Love,
Grandpa

WEDNESDAY, APRIL 26, 1995

Driving while Sleepy

To Ryan:

Sources tell me that you already have and are using your driver's license. Congratulations! Grandma Loe got her license before she was sixteen, too. She practiced in the pasture in western Kansas. She's a great driver—better than I am, by far. To illustrate: We were driving down to Florida. We had picked up Uncle Rob and your mom from Saturday catechism class and took off. Grandma and I alternated driving every couple of hours. To save time and expense, we had decided to drive straight through to my folks' home in Winter Park, Florida. It was 3:00 a.m. in Georgia, and my turn to drive. Uncle Charlie, Uncle Rob, and your mom were in the back seat. I was sleepy but continued to drive. I awoke to a loud grinding noise and showers of sparks. We had drifted into the concrete wall of a bridge in the Okefenokee Swamp. I recovered, stopped at the side of the road off the bridge, and shook! Thinking of what could have happened scared us all to death! Thanks to God, I am here today.

Love,
Grandpa

Be Flexible

To Ryan:

Did you know that I graduated from West Point? Well, not the regular West Point. It seems that the regular cadets did not use their airfield, planes, or instructors during the winter months, when they attended regular classes. They used them summertime only. A bunch of us "aviation cadets" were sent there to make use of the facilities. After awhile, the instructors really lauded us. They said that the West Pointers were so rigidly schooled and disciplined that they were inflexible. On cross-country trips, when the West Pointers encountered icing conditions at altitudes or conditions conducive to icing, they would remain at the scheduled altitude no matter what. A number of them had been lost or killed when they "spun in." We had to learn logic and common sense—and survived! Be flexible. Use your brain.

Love,
Grandpa

WEDNESDAY, MAY 10, 1995

Union Negotiations

To Ryan:

Negotiations during the baseball strike took me back to my days of negotiations with the factory unions. I probably attended union negotiations for thirty years. The company's tactic (all three companies I worked for had the same format) was to have only one spokesman. He was generally a lawyer from headquarters. Even when questions were directed to others, he answered to make sure it followed our plan of action. The union was not always so disciplined. Everyone "on the other side of the table" chipped in from time to time. As I later learned, the real negotiations took place at breakfast, between our lawyer and the union's international rep, who was their titular head. All the rest, when the rest of us were present, was "window dressing" for the union membership. The results were amicable and mutually satisfactory. Too bad the baseball "non-contract" negotiations weren't.

Love,
Grandpa

Cross-Stitching

To Ryan:

Just as I did for you and all our grandchildren, I'm cross-stitching a baby quilt for your newest cousin, Jess Higgins. I go way back, to when we were just married, with cross-stitching. We've still got my first project. We saw a poem at Zinck's, a bar, while at Cornell. I copied it, and later cross-stitched it for our apartment wall. Couldn't afford much more then. SEVILLE DER DAGO—TOUSEN BUZES INA ROE—NO JO DEMIS TRUX—VOTSINNEM COUSEN DUX. I don't know whether or not your mom remembers it. Can you figure it out yourself? You might wonder why I got into cross-stitching anyway. I guess as an engineer, it is more or less symmetrical and repetitive, yet artistic in its own way. It is creative. It certainly slows me down, to cause me to rest and relax a bit, as an alternate hobby and accomplishment. It is fun, and something you all can enjoy and remember.

Love,
Grandpa

WEDNESDAY, JUNE 7, 1995

Summertime in Milwaukee

To Ryan:

Summertime! That's always meant bare feet to me. Growing up on the south side of Milwaukee, we kids looked forward to it. I liked school, but the summer break was a welcome relief. Except for church on Sunday, we didn't use shoes. Our feet bottoms were tough as nails after a couple of weeks. Then, we had a lot of tarry streets and repairs. It was fun popping the tar bubbles that rose in the summer heat.

The ice man came around in a horse-pulled wagon, his ice blocks covered with sawdust to slow melting. His customers placed a card showing 25-50-75-100 to designate the number of pounds they wanted. He'd chink off small pieces of ice for the kids, after delivering.

Somebody had a bat and ball, so we'd choose sides and play ball in the empty lot in the next block. To see who would pick first, one would hold the bat by its end hub while the other would try to kick it off.

Love,
Grandpa

Spanking

To Ryan:

There's a big hullabaloo (it's in the dictionary!) these days over harassment and abuse. It seems that there's a fine line between abuse and punishment. I'm sure that I was spanked when I was a youngster. As I got older, my dad didn't have to spank me—a stern look or "dressing down" kept me more in line. When RRCB (Rob, Ris, Charlie, and Barb) came along, I spanked. One day I asked my mom, who was visiting, why little Rob looked so terrified as I approached him to "discipline" him. She said, "Think how you'd feel if a person three times your size came at you with that "look" in his eyes. How'd you react?" Right then, I made a new rule! Since most problems arose between siblings, I'd have the offender bend over, grab ankles, and await a swat from the other. If both were at fault, both would administer a swat to each other. It worked! I think it did. Ask your mom.

Love,
Grandpa

WEDNESDAY, JUNE 21, 1995

Everything Comes from God

To Ryan:

Last Sunday the priest quoted an old philosopher saying, "Work as though everything depended on you; pray as though everything depended on God." That work part is particularly true when it comes to teamwork. You could apply that to your team sports, too. Last week in the NBA Finals, Olajuwon, the MVP, apparently took it to heart, and won. But even he needed the rest of the team, and teamwork, to sweep the Orlando Magic in four. I'm sure the coaches will emphasize that in your summer camps and next fall. 'Course, your "team" at 309 Canary Lane is expecting that you'll apply yourself at school, too. And, you know, that latter part about God is meaningful, too. We all like to think that all our accomplishments are the result of our own selves. Hold it! Everything, I mean *everything*, ultimately comes from God.

Love,
Grandpa

Wearing a Bow Tie

To Ryan:

Do you remember ever seeing me wearing a long straight tie? I was trying to remember the last time that I did. I think that I wore a bow tie in college for a while, although we seldom wore ties there. On the other hand, my entire senior year at Cornell I wore long ties. That was to get used to wearing a shirt, tie, and coat in preparation for interviewing for a job, and for undoubtedly wearing one daily after I did get a job in industry. They were always regular, standard, long, straight ties. I felt comfortable in them. Along about five or ten years before I retired I guess I got back on the bow tie "kick." It was probably one of those "be different—don't be one of the herd" kind of things that didn't hurt anyone, and I really didn't have to worry about my image anymore. That is, it was an expression of independence and individuality. It was great for a tall guy like me, and I still think they look neat!

Love,
Grandpa

A Young Man at War

To Ryan:

Here's the ole flag waver again. 'Course, we fly the flag every day, not just on July Fourth. And when I see a flag in a parade, or sing America or the National Anthem, I get pumped up and exhilarated. When I went overseas in January, 1945, I was a typical young man going to war— patriotic, adventuresome, anxious, and ready to fight. In battle, in the Air Force (Army Air Corps in those days) it was exciting: flak (black bursts in the air around the plane), Bettys and Zeros (Japanese twin- and single-engine fighters) driving at, shooting at, and colliding with planes in the sky. There was too much happening to really get scared at the moment. After twenty or more missions, our crew flew back to California from Tinian for lead crew training. Soon as I could, I saw Grandma Loe. When I had to go back overseas, it was the hardest thing I'd ever had to do. Thankfully, the war was over weeks later.

Love,
Grandpa

The Platinum Rule

To Ryan:

You've heard of one-up-manship—that is, when someone tries to, or does, outperform another person. It can be in sports, business, family, or the political arena. Well, I recently heard that against, would you believe, the Golden Rule? This person asked if anyone had heard of the Platinum Rule. Platinum being more precious than gold, I figured that there couldn't be a better philosophy to live by than the Golden Rule, "Do unto others as you would have others do unto you." He quoted this: "Do unto others as you think others would like to be treated" as the Platinum Rule. There is a significant difference, isn't there? I think that the Platinum Rule is better than the Golden Rule because it's based on the other guy's priorities, instead of ours. Think about it.

Love,
Grandpa

Meeting Grandma

To Ryan:

You have another Higgins cousin—Jake (James Michael Barry) was born Sunday morning. He looks just like Brian did at birth. We met him for the first time Sunday night, on arrival in Wisconsin. Can you remember the first time you met certain friends and relatives? I met Grandma Loe on July 25, 1944. In Grand Island, Nebraska, to begin training with a crew for overseas combat service, I went swimming at the city pool. After spotting this beautiful young lady on the opposite side of the pool, I dove in. I swam underwater across the width of the pool. On coming up right at the place she was sitting with her sister, Carole, wise-guy, cocky old me said, "Hi, what's your name?" Reluctantly, she finally said, "Smith." "Sure," I said, "and mine is Jones!" (Her maiden name really was Smith!) Well, the rest is history. We got together for a date. Next year it will be our fiftieth anniversary!

Love,
Grandpa

The 1-2-3 Program

To Ryan:

Frequently, I get good inspirational ideas at Sunday Mass and the sermon. Whenever I used to give speeches, lectures, or talks, I tried to provide some substance for the listeners to take home and use in their lives and work. Last Sunday the priest gave me substance. He suggested a 1-2-3 program each day.

1. Review all that you enjoyed or experienced for the day, and thank God for that.
2. Review all your errors and wrongs against others during the day, and tell God that you are sorry and ask for forgiveness.
3. Review that which is ahead in the future or planned for, and ask God for help in accomplishing it all.

The 1-2-3 (thank-sorry-help) program sounds pretty good to me! 'Course, it can be weekly rather than daily. I'm going to try it. Why don't you? It will make each of us a better person. Think about it.

Love,
Grandpa

WEDNESDAY, AUGUST 9, 1995

Muroc Army Air Base

To Ryan:

It's hot! It's in the high nineties and has been over one hundred degrees at times. We're sort of used to that in Kansas City. On the other hand, we'd send workers home in Milwaukee when the temperature went over ninety-five. In Independence, it's said that you should have air conditioning at home, at the office, and in the car in order to survive. The hottest that I can remember was during the war in 1945. We had come back from combat after some twenty-plus missions over Japan. Our crew was designated a lead crew. We were to train so that we could lead a squadron of B-29s in bombing raids, called pattern bombing, as they had done in Europe. We'd "practice bomb" Los Angeles and San Francisco. It was cool at altitude. When we landed and were taxiing in, I'd throw open my hatch window. It was like a furnace. We were in Muroc Army Air Base in the California desert.

Love,
Grandpa

Making up Your Mind

To Ryan:

Have you ever been in a situation where you can't make up your mind—which movie to go to, what book to read, or which job or chore to tackle first? I have. It's perplexing. I've a solution; someone suggested it to me years ago. It seems to work. You flip a coin. Now it's not so simple as that, however. To really find out what you'd really rather do, the secret is what happens after you've flipped the coin. If you say, prior to the flip, heads, I do "A," tails, I do "B," it sets the stage. Now, if either heads or tails turns up, and down deep you feel disappointed, you know that you'd really rather do the other alternative than the one turned up! Get it? Try it! I've a corollary to that scenario, too. Talking to someone about alternatives, I ask, "Would you like to do 'A'?" If they hesitate a long time, I say "You've flipped the coin on me!"—meaning that they would rather do "B" but are afraid to say so.

Love,
Grandpa

WEDNESDAY, SEPTEMBER 6, 1995

Cal Ripken and Lou Gehrig

To Ryan:

I was really impressed last week seeing Cal Ripken Jr. We were at a KC Royals game against Baltimore. He seemed like an ordinary guy. He played and batted well. He signed autographs for as many as requested. Today, he will beat the consecutive-games-played record of Lou Gehrig; 2,130 games . . . fantastic. What a role model for all athletes, not just baseball players. 'Course, we've heard all about this for quite awhile. His work ethic is unusual in these times. They erected a memorial to Lou Gehrig in Yankee Stadium, thinking that Gehrig's feat would never be exceeded. Wow! Cal played through injuries, hangovers, batting slumps, frustrations, and attitudes. He had a job to do every day. He showed up for work, to work. He trained in and out of season. He came to work hours before teammates to practice and perfect his skills. He made the most use of his God-given talents. Yet, he is reportedly a humble, gracious, polite, family man, and doggedly competitive. I wish I could be more like him.

Love,
Grandpa

Keeping a Streak Going

To Ryan:

Well, Cal Ripken Jr. has his streak. He'll probably continue . . . maybe all the way up to 3,000. Good luck and best wishes to him. Closer to home . . . I've got my streak going. My Wednesday letters began when you became a teenager. It will continue until you are eighteen years old. You might wonder how I keep it without repeats. I caught myself awhile back doing just that. One's memory falters with age. So, I devised a system of cross-referenced files to cover that eventuality. I use my twilight time (about three or four o'clock every morning) to do some of my best planning, inventing, recollecting, and thinking. Subjects for the Wednesday letters often come up for consideration. I've got a list built up so I'll never run out till you're eighteen. I try to keep a little in reserve at all times in everything that I do. We'll talk about that later.

Love,
Grandpa

WEDNESDAY, SEPTEMBER 20, 1995

Proper Grammar

To Ryan:

When meeting all of your teachers at school the other night, I was reminded of my own time in school. My mom was a schoolteacher, too. I always had trouble with my grammar and use of personal pronouns, "I" and "me." She helped in getting my speech correct. Dad was an attorney and a stickler for that and my spelling, too. It was better and less embarrassing for them to point out my misgivings than teachers. By the time I got to college, and the real world of business afterward, I was in pretty ship-shape condition. I was surprised to see presentations and applications from people. How'd they ever get out of high school? They tell me that it's no better nowadays. Mom's simple rule was: put the other person's name or reference first, followed by the proper "I" or "me." She said: start out with "Bob and I did this" and end with "It was a gift to Bob and me." Think it over. Some simple, but effective rules of thumb.

Love,
Grandpa

Keeping a Little Bit in Reserve

To Ryan:

Grandma and I had our annual physical exams lately. The doctor told both of us that we were in relatively good health. We asked about our weights. He said that we were above average for our age in weight; perhaps in the upper level of the range. However, he said you want to be in that situation because the older you get, you are more susceptible to disease and you should have a "little bit" in reserve. I chuckled, because that's my own philosophy in most scenarios. Financially, too many times people invest all of their capital in some venture without any reserve. Then, as unforeseen problems arise, they have no back-up or reserve. They lose it all. Athletically, a team puts on a full court press or eleven-man rushing blitz, and a quick pass gets down court or down the field. They're dead. They should've kept a "little bit" in reserve. Does that all make sense? Sure, you work, invest, and play to the best of your abilities, but your adrenaline is your "little bit" in reserve.

Love,
Grandpa

Understanding Sin

To Ryan:

Do you know what a sin is? The dictionary says that a sin is an offense against God, or His commandments. I've always thought that it would be difficult for one person to tell whether or not another person had committed a sin. To me, a person must acknowledge to himself that what is about to or has happened is wrong. Who knows what a person is thinking, down deep within. 'Course, an acknowledged wrong against another person is really against God (or one of God's creatures). Mahatma Gandhi once listed seven deadly "sins":

1. Wealth without work
2. Pleasure without conscience
3. Knowledge without character
4. Commerce without morality
5. Science without humanity
6. Worship without sacrifice
7. Politics without principle

That's pretty heavy, isn't it? I guess that I like simple rules and laws. I figured my mom and dad were God's "agents," and my best "guide" was to ask myself: "what would Mom and Dad (God) think or say about my action?"

Love,
Grandpa

134

Finding a Pilot's Remains

To Ryan:

Time for another war story! Fate and coincidence figure into this one. A guy named Joe was a roommate in Basic Flight Training at Sumter Air Field in South Carolina. We had all soloed, but Joe needed practice on his high performance climbing turns. His instructor checked Joe out one day, then sent him solo to practice. Next we heard, a farmer had a "crazy" plane "land" in his pasture—with no pilot. Logic told us Joe had spun, bailed out, hit his tail empennage before his parachute opened, and was probably buried in the Okefenokee Swamp outside town. We had hundreds of infantry help us cadets comb the swamp, arm to arm. No luck! Time passes. In 1955, twelve years later, I went on a trip to a paper company in Massachusetts as quality control manager for my company. At lunch with our supplier, we talked about our wartime experiences. Coincidentally, the paper executive had been a pilot at Sumter, too, but later than me. He told of a New York Times article that week that retold of the finding of the skeletal remains of a pilot the swamp had disgorged—my former roommate, Joe!

Love,
Grandpa

Using a Beautiful Shotgun

To Ryan:

We heard about your going out hunting again. It reminded me of my first hunting trip. My boss was a hunter. He and I had talked about it often. It was no surprise, then, when I was promoted to our largest plant, that my fellow staff members gave me a fourteen-gauge shotgun as a going away present. It was a Remington pump. It was and still is a beautiful gun. Shortly after, we were spending Thanksgiving in Hill City, Kansas with Bobye and Buck, Grandma Loe's sister and brother-in-law. Naturally, I took my shotgun out with us. Buck promised good hunting in western Kansas on their farm property. We went out the first morning. During the day, in the woods, along the railroad tracks, and in the hedgerows I managed to get six squirrels, six rabbits, and six quail. Buck did even better. Buck commented, "You'll always enjoy hunting from now on—even if you don't get any during a particular shoot!" He was certainly right. I do. May you continue to have good hunting.

Love,

Grandpa

Being a Competitor

To Ryan:

How competitive are you? What kind of a competitor are you? The reason I ask is that one of my racquetball partners told me about a movie he and his son had recently seen. I'm going to get a video copy to watch, to get my own reaction. It's *Days of Thunder,* or something similar. It's about car racing. A driver and some mechanics left a team owner and his crew to start their own team. At an important title race, the driver lost an engine. He and his crew were short of money. His mechanic suddenly appeared with a new engine. When asked as to how he had gotten it, he said that he had "stolen" it. Actually, it seems, the old owner had given it to him. Then, during the race, the driver and his crew had starter trouble, so the owner told his own crew to go out and help push the car onto the track. The point of the whole story being that, to be really competitive, to be a good competitor is to know that you've really beaten the best and you help your competition to be its best. Think about it.

Love,
Grandpa

Receiving Compliments

To Ryan:

How often have you been around anyone getting a gift and witnessing a stammered, sometimes inaudible response? Words like, "Aw, you shouldn't have done that or gotten that for me!" are commonplace in such situations. Probably one of the most difficult characteristics to display and cultivate is that of accepting gifts, compliments, and favors graciously. It's surprising how well-received a simple "Thank you" and "That was nice of you" to the donor is appreciated. Too often, the effusive response makes for an awkward or embarrassing situation to both the donor and the donee. I have difficulty following my own suggestion at times because I want to do nice things for other people, without being rewarded or acknowledged in return. Giving compliments is difficult for some people. I enjoy it. For yourself, try accepting and giving in a straightforward way— look them in the eye, give a clear response or statement, and smile. Think about it.

Love,
Grandpa

Considering College

To Ryan:

Have you thought about college yet? Last Sunday's paper had articles about that. They say that it isn't too early to think about going to college . . . even in your early high school career. Seems to me that it was when I was a junior in high school when my buddies and I talked about it. All the crowd that I ran around with were jocks and good students. As it turned out, all of them went to college—even though it was interrupted by having to go to war. Some of them had money problems. I was one of those. We chose smaller, less expensive colleges and applied for scholarships to help pay the way. We had college entrance exams then. You all call them SATs and other names, now. I applied at Lehigh, Cornell, Stanford, MIT, and Georgia Tech. Besides good test scores and good grades, extracurricular sports, clubs, projects, and personal interviews were important. I wonder what I would have done without college. Think about it.

Love,
Grandpa

Traveling Is in Our Family

To Ryan:

We love to travel, Grandma Loe and me! 'Course, during World War II, I flew around the states for training and cross-country flights to Cuba and then to Hawaii, Kwajalain, Euiwetok, Guam, Saipan, and Tinian in the Pacific. After the war, my industrial career took us around the US again, and to Europe and South America. The companies I worked for would include Grandma if it were a convention or dealer award trips. During vacations, the family went by car: north, south, east, and west. The travel bug is in the family. Your mom and Uncle Rob bussed around the US one summer visiting relatives on both sides of the country. Then the two of them went to Germany alone on a Rotary exchange project. We all picked them up and toured Europe afterward. Uncle Charlie attended mime training in Paris. Interestingly, since retirement, we haven't ventured offshore. However, all our friends in Independence nicknamed us "The Gypsies" because of our trips, even now.

Love,
Grandpa

You Are Uniquely Made

To Ryan:

Did you ever realize that there is only one being in the world like you? You are unique! Besides the fact that humans are different from plants and animals, besides the fact that fingerprints of every human are different, besides the fact that you look a lot like your father and have many characteristics of your mother, you are the only person exactly like you. You may imitate good traits and skills of your idols and mentors. You may get instructions from your parents, teachers, coaches, or friends. You may be part of a group or liken yourself to others. The fact remains that you are one unto yourself. Be proud of that! Consider that God has given you some clay and wood to sculpt into a finished product that will be pleasing to Him, to yourself, and to all others. A cut here, a notch there, some smoothing and blending, shades of color and hues, a sprinkling of humor, and an energy that can accomplish anything the mind is set to do. Know that He and I are always with you.

Love,
Grandpa

WEDNESDAY, DECEMBER 20, 1995

Do the Unexpected

To Ryan:

Today is your Uncle Rob's birthday. We are lucky enough to have him visiting us here in Florida. He, Susan, Grandma, and I will celebrate Christmas together next Monday. Merry Christmas to you! I'm wearing one red sock and one green sock everyday till then. I'm wearing a big furry red and white Santa hat, too. I wear it out to the stores and restaurants, and I wish everyone a merry Christmas when I meet them in the street or in the stores and malls. Grandma gets a little embarrassed, but everyone smiles and greets me back! Reminds me of a season years ago. I was giving an important speech to the president of Allis-Chalmers. I wore a loud, colorful tie that Grandma had made, showing holly leaves and big red poinsettia flowers. As I greeted Mr. Scott, he remarked on my "nice-looking Christmas tie." I promptly took it off and gave it to him. Then, I whipped out a regular tie from my pocket and put it on, and proceeded with my speech. Everyone laughed, including Mr. Scott. Everyone remembered. Within reason, it pays to do the unexpected. Think about it.

Love,
Grandpa

How to Manage Your Time

To Ryan:

Time! There's just not enough time, never enough hours in a day to do all the things there are to do. How did I spend ten or more hours a day at the plant and get things done at home before I retired? A lot of retirees experience the same scenario! 'Course, I do read more of the newspaper, do more crossword puzzles, play more golf and racquetball, pay more attention to our investment portfolio and opportunities, watch a little more TV, and help Grandma with chores more than before. It all comes down to budgeting available time, planning work, and working the plan. At work, and in retirement, too, I considered my time as money. Sure, I wasted some time or "money". And, I "spent" some time, or "money," relaxing. But then, and even now, most of my time was used in preparation and execution of meaningful productive work and action—then for my family and career, now for my family and health—be it physical, mental, spiritual, material, or psychological.

Love,
Grandpa

DATE Wednesday 04/03/96

To: Ryan —

DATE Wednesday 07/31/96

To: Ryan —

MEMORANDUM

Grandma and I are going out to Kay Wiggins
wedding in Lake Tahoe tomorrow. That and our
recent anniversary reminds me of our wedding/
honeymoon. We were married in Grand Island, Neb.
We rented a seclusive cabin in the Colorado
mountains for our honeymoon. The ___

DATE Wednesday 04/10/96

MEMORANDUM

___ careful? Course, I'm careful grandpa
___ what you do, in how you act, and

DATE Wednesday 03/06/96

MEMORANDUM

DATE Wednesday 05/15/96

To: Ryan —

MEMORANDUM

Be prepared, the motto of the Boy Scouts.
Upon a time, I was a Boy Scout, thought
beyond first class. I always wished that
gone on and become an Eagle Scout. ___
something, I would be really proud of ___
But — back to my news. Be prepared
when you get to college sports you ___
drugs and illegal subst___
to know all about that, first hand ___
going out or part of a crew to test ___
for drugs/substances for the NCAA ___

DATE Wednesday 00/02/96

To: Ryan —

MEMORANDUM

In my new work in SCORE counselling people
starting their own business, it brings back
memories I guess everyone, at one time or
another thinks about going into business for them___
I know that I did — more than once! A combin___
of hearing/investigating about a business for ___
or of starting a new one and a time when my
industrial/corporate job had lost its challeng___

1996

Wednesday, January 10, 1996

Responsibility

To Ryan:

A combine is a complicated machine. It is part truck, part grain cutter, part grain gatherer, part thresher, part grain and chaff separator, part grain storage, and part transfer unit. It's a combination of all of these, hence the name. Every part of the combine has its own blueprint. Many, many other prints show how all these are assembled together to form a finished machine product. What brought all that to mind was the space launch of Endeavor going up tomorrow morning. When I had the responsibility of producing combines, I knew that a malfunction would cause an irate customer or a broken-down combine to raise Cain. That's "peanuts" when one considers what a poor-quality or bad electronic or mechanical part might do to a space flight. It can be deadly, as was the case with the Challenger. The lives of astronauts and families can be changed forever. The responsibility must be awesome. Think about it. What a challenge!

Love,

Grandpa

Discipline Is Key

To Ryan:

The news of Jimmy Johnson, new coach of the Dolphins, and a biography of General Schwartzkopf on TV brought to mind the subject of discipline. Jimmy Johnson isn't particularly well thought of, as opposed to General Schwartzkopf, who is allegedly well-liked. Yet both of them are known for their characteristic of discipline. Discipline was drilled into me in the service. At the time, I didn't like it or understand it, but went along because it was part of being a soldier. After awhile, I grew to really respect it, during pilot training and especially during combat. After the war, I realized its importance to me personally again during college, and then in the workplace. 'Course, self-discipline is primary. You plan your work, then work your plan to your and everyone's benefit. It's tough sometimes. When you're a manager or a leader, discipline is key. Think about it.

Love,
Grandpa

WEDNESDAY, JANUARY 24, 1996

Sneaking a Smoke

To Ryan:

You know, moms are pretty shrewd "old birds," aren't they? My mom was. One day, our parochial school had a day off. All my buddies were in public school. My classmates were busy elsewhere. Playing around by my brother Ed's room, I came across his pipe. He'd have me fill it for him before smoking, so I knew the technique. Mom was downstairs. I figured that I'd try to smoke a pipe myself. I loaded it and lit it, coughing a bit along the way. For a sub-teen like me, it was exhilarating. Then I started feeling a bit woozy. I quickly put it out and replaced the pipe after emptying it, all the while feeling worse. I opened the window to let the smoke out and hurried downstairs. I told Mom that I didn't feel well. She must have smelled the smoke. I'm sure I reeked of it. She just said, "That's too bad, honey. Here, take a spoonful of this castor oil!" Two inches away, I threw up. Think about it.

Love,
Grandpa

Poor Career Choice

To Ryan:

Today is Grandma Loe's birthday. She's thirty-nine and counting! We'll celebrate by opening some presents, some wine, and having dinner out with friends, probably at Patrick Air Force Base next door. A friend is a retired Army officer. Reminds me of my poor decision years ago. During World War II service, I was classified as a four-engine bomber pilot, B-29 with a MOS (military occupational status) of 1095. I left the Army Air Force in 1945 with the rank of first lieutenant. After graduating from Cornell in February 1949, BME, I retained the reserve rank of first lieutenant. Figuring that I'd rather "fly" a desk on the next war, I requested and received a change of MOS to purchasing and productive control officer. Rather than spending one weekend a month and two weekends each summer in reserve training, I resigned my reserve commission. I could be enjoying a pension, base privileges, and colonel's rank now in the reserves. Bad decision then. Think about it.

Love,
Grandpa

Liberal vs. Conservative

To Ryan:

Your Grandpa Pearce is conservative . . . and I guess I am also a conservative. Nowadays, everyone is talking about *the* conservatives in Congress. My dad was a Democrat and my mom was a Republican. 'Course, about the time that I was growing up, there was the Great Depression, in the late twenties and thirties. My dad believed that Franklin Delano Roosevelt could bring the USA out of the depression . . . actually he put into effect the things that Herbert Hoover had envisioned. They were the archetypal liberal Democrat and conservative Republican. The two political parties have changed a lot, but they are basically still liberal versus conservative—big government taking care of all the social needs (perceived) of the people versus less government (federal as opposed to states) allowing entrepreneurial ingenuity and ambition to fend for themselves and succeed or fail, as the case may be. Are you thinking as a liberal or a conservative? Do you know what your family's positions are? Think and talk about it.

Love,
Grandpa

Playing Many Sports

To Ryan:

Uncle Rob tells me that you'll be visiting Santa Fe, Albuquerque, and New Mexico University soon. What's the attraction? Wrestling? You really have the muscles, physique, and perseverance to be good at wrestling. Let's see—it's football in the fall, wrestling in the winter, and track in the spring? 'Course, studies all school year long, too. Go for it! What do you do in track? It still amazes me to see hurdles—I guess it's because I'd have so much trouble getting my long legs up for a hurdle. Do they include hurdles in the pentathlon? Do they have that multi-event at Bozeman High? Have you ever tried them? Seems to me that you'd excel at such events. With all the attributes described above for you, how about it? Don't need to win each event, but why not?

Love,

Grandpa

Professional Engineer's Organization

To Ryan:

A couple of Canadians working for me talked about a professional engineer's organization in Canada. About all graduate engineers there, on graduation, are members. They wear an iron ring as members. Great idea. So, I adapted and created my own: BAR. That is an acronym for Band and Ring. It is for engineers in the US who have passed their professional engineer's exam. I copyrighted and patented the pledge (band) and design on the ring of sterling silver with intersecting lines symbolizing lines used by engineers on graphs, plots, tables, surveys, and designs. The band, as opposed to the Canadians' or the Bible, is couched in positive terms, such as "Thou shall" rather than "Thou shall not," in dealing with the ethics for an engineer doing his work for the public, his company, and himself. The ring is worn on the little finger of the right hand, denoting a marriage to one's profession, similar to a wedding ring.

Love,

Grandpa

Choosing a College

To Ryan:

The word's out that University of New Mexico has been scratched from your list of potential colleges. Wherever you decide, are you going to try for a scholarship? We "talked" about my getting one for Cornell before, but did I ever tell you that I was awarded two? After hearing from Lehigh that I won a full four-year scholarship, I replied, thanking them for the honor. The next week I received word from Cornell—again, a full year "ride." I was in a dilemma. I had tested for both and liked both. I asked my dad what to do! He said that both were good engineering schools. He said that I could become a good engineer graduating from either school, or, for that matter, from about any school that taught from similar books, if I applied myself. However, he opined that Cornell carried a slightly better name and image in industry. I chose Cornell . . . but it is the student, not the school, that counts in the end.

Love,
Grandpa

Forming an Honorary Society

To Ryan:

Your grandpa believes in "making his own breaks," in forging new trails, and in taking advantage of a situation, all for the betterment of self and society. Case in point: At Cornell there are honorary societies, as at most colleges. It so happened that all the other engineering colleges at Cornell (civil, electrical, chemical) had academic honorary societies, besides the social honoraries, except the Sibley School of Mechanical Engineering. We were the largest, yet we weren't represented. I deemed to change that! After some research, inquiries, calls, correspondence, and faculty coaching, I organized a group of my classmates who could meet the requirements of a national, recognized, prestigious honorary society for mechanical engineers: Pi Tau Sigma. We did it! I was classified as founder and first president. It was a tremendous feeling of satisfaction and accomplishment. Pi Tau Sigma exists on the Cornell campus today as one of the elite. All it took was "guts." Think about it.

Love,
Grandpa

Thoughts, Words, Actions, Habits, and Character

To Ryan:

Are you careful? "'Course I'm careful, Grandpa," you say. In what you do, how you act, and in how you react, I'm sure that you are. If, by chance, something unexpected happens, you're quick enough, strong enough, and smart enough to compensate and recover. I ran across a little quip the other day to carry that further:

Be careful of your thoughts,
For your thoughts become your words.
Be careful of your words,
For your words become your actions.
Be careful of your actions,
For your actions become your habits.
Be careful of your habits,
For your habits become your character.
Be careful of your character,
For your character becomes your destiny.

Can't claim authorship . . . wish I could. Think about it.

Love,
Grandpa

Fleeting Fame

To Ryan:

Heard a sad story recently: A local high school athlete was an all-conference ball player. All his fellow students and teachers praised him. The coeds dated him. The local businesses feted him during the season. He was a senior. Then, an interesting development took place. After the season ended, his invites and dates stopped. He couldn't understand it. Finally, he realized that his "fame" was a fleeting thing. People had used him. Naturally, he was embittered . . . can you blame him? Reminds me of a friend in Zanesville. He was president of a pottery firm—a "big man in town." Suddenly, the owners of the company decided to close shop. My friend was devastated. He told me that people had crossed the street to shake his hand in the past. Now, they were crossing the street to avoid him. People realized he no longer was a person of influence—no use to them. He took it personally. I tried to convey that that wasn't so. Think about it!

Love,
Grandpa

Setting Limits

To Ryan:

It's fun sometimes to know something about your parents when they were young. Doubt that your mom has forgotten this incident, though. She's probably put it away—way back in her memory bank. Children challenge parents at times, really to set limits on their own behavior. It's easier to act out than to talk out when you're young, impressionable, and aggressive. In this instance, the family had gone to the Milwaukee airport administration building (old one on Layton Avenue) to watch airplanes and to check schedules. On leaving, I got the car from the parking lot. I drove around the semicircle drive to pick up everyone. Everyone got in the car, except your mom. She, for some reason, was not going to get in at that time. We cajoled, coaxed, and finally threatened her to get in. Still, no! So I said, "OK, then we'll just leave you here." I drove off. 'Course, I just went around the semicircle, but a weeping, contrite little girl finally got in.

Love,
Grandpa

Drug-Testing Athletes

To Ryan:

"Be prepared."—the motto of the Boy Scouts. Once upon a time, I was a Boy Scout, though I never got beyond first class. I always wished that I had gone on to become an Eagle Scout. That would be something I would be really proud of attaining. But back to my news. Be prepared—cause when you get to college sports you will be tested; that is, for drugs and illegal substances. I'm going to know all about that, firsthand. Today, I'm going out as part of a crew to test athletes for drugs and illegal substances for the NCAA. The crew chief is Teresa Hopper Reilly, daughter of Chuck Hopper, my golfing partner, and best friend of your Aunt Barb. We are a crew of four or five. We're going in completely unannounced at an NCAA tournament. My job will be to monitor the randomly selected athletes as they go through urinalysis tests for substance abuse. Anyone who tests positive will have any records and performance negated for that particular tournament. It could cost the school a title, championship, or tournament. I'll report back next week on results

Love,
Grandpa

Athletic Drug-Testing Procedure

To Ryan:

Back from my NCAA trip last week. We went to Portland, Maine, to the University of South Maine. We hit the coaches meeting when we got in Wednesday night. The baseball championship for District 3A was to begin the next day. It was a double elimination tournament. The coaches weren't particularly surprised. They accepted our presence with equanimity. We got to watch Bridgeport defeat Brandeis, six to two, the next day. Then we randomly selected six of the twenty-three on each squad for testing. They were a great bunch of athletes. As a monitor and validator, you couldn't touch them, their clothes, their drink, their canister or cup, or their paperwork. We talked them through getting their sterile cup into the "john," stripping to the waist, dropping all lower clothing to below their knees, rotating 360 degrees, urinating, and back out to our paperwork people. Some were, like me, "BBs" (bashful bladders), but we talked them out of that. No one will know the results till after the lab checks.

Love,
Grandpa

WEDNESDAY, MAY 29, 1996

Earning Letters

To Ryan:

I hope that you don't mind, but your mom shared some of your wisdom with us the other day. After telling us of your triple jump personal best and getting to go to state meet, we were jubilant. Then she told us about the lessons you've learned during the school year in your three sports: from football, leadership; from wrestling, discipline; and from track, willpower! That so impressed us that I wrote it down, just to comment on it and to congratulate you on your insight. That is great. Then, following that, she told us that, by getting to state, you qualify for a third letter in sports at Bozeman High. How proud we are of you and your accomplishments! While checking results of your state meet today with Joe, he absolutely flabbergasted me when he reported what had happened at the Sports Banquet. The only underclassman and only one of three, out of a school of 1,400, to be honored with three letters is incredible! That's *determination*. We love you

Love,
Grandpa

Cheering for Ryan

To Ryan:

"Don't let yesterday use up too much of today!" Good ole
boy philosopher made that statement. Don't dwell on the
past—put any mistake behind you. Use the past experience
to better your future plans. 'Course, that goes for the glory,
too—don't dwell on it. And, don't let others take up your
time or energy, cause you are going to be concentrating on
next year and the future, setting and meeting new goals
and objectives. On the other hand, we're your team of
cheerleaders. I've devised a cheer, the "roar": RRR (rally
'round Ryan!). No cheerleaders at wrestling or track, but
for football, we'll roar RRR! (Only with your permission!)
We're going to get to Bozeman this fall. Spent a day in May
painting. A group from Rotary got together and painted a
whole house in one day for a needy family. We descended
like the proverbial "herd of turtles." It was amazing how
well and fast it went. The house looked great; the family was
overjoyed; and we all felt pleased at having done something
for someone in need. How are your RAKs (random acts of
kindness) coming? I try for one a day. Tough, but I try.

Love,

Grandpa

Rocky Mountain Oysters

To Ryan:

Have you ever heard of Rocky Mountain Oysters? When Grandma Loe was growing up on a Kansas ranch, they would prepare meals for the harvest hands. Often they served "mountain oysters" (actually the fried testicles of sheep). They are delicious, but to the uninitiated, they sound uninviting. One new worker really enjoyed the meal—even asked for seconds. However, on inquiry, and finding out what they were, he promptly excused himself, beat it to behind the barn, and threw up. True story. It does remind me of another that I just heard. Seems a visitor to Mexico had heard about this dive with great "mountain oysters." He ordered some. They were huge—and delicious. On asking their source, the waiter explained that there was a bullring right next door and that they were bull's testicles. The next day, the stranger returned. He again ordered mountain oysters. They were tiny. He asked the waiter, "How come the other day they were huge?" The waiter replied, "Sometimes the bull wins!"

Love,
Grandpa

Custom Wheat Cutters

To Ryan:

About this time, or perhaps later, you'll see the wheat fields of Montana being harvested. There are teams of workers, called "custom cutters," that cut and deliver the golden wheat to the storage silos for farmers that can't afford or don't want to mess with the combines and related equipment. These "cutters" work on "piecework," or incentives that involve formulas to determine the costs and price for the harvesting work. Generally, the "code" involves three identical numbers, such as 20-20-20. This means the cutters are paid by the farmer: twenty dollars per acre cut, twenty cents per bushel to haul the wheat to the "elevators" for storage, and twenty cents per bushel for all yield over thirty bushels per acre. Depending on the price of wheat on the commodities exchange (where they buy and sell wheat) and the number of jobs that the cutter has lined up, the job can be 14-14-14 or 25-25-25 negotiated price. The cutters start in Texas in mid-May and progress up to Canada in late August. A cutter can make big bucks. He has to pay up to $150,000 or more for a combine. You might "hire on" a crew next year. Think about it.

Love,
Grandpa

Family Reunion and 50th Anniversary

To Ryan:

We're really going to have to squeeze in a lot of talking and doing, the seventeen of us, next week. Time will go by so fast that it will seem as though we'll all be saying good-bye just after saying hello. Thank you for taking the time to come to our fiftieth wedding anniversary and reunion celebration in Florida. Years ago, a neighbor of ours, anticipating a trip to New York City, asked my mom and dad to suggest places and things to do while in NYC. He knew that they were well-traveled and knowledgeable. They pointed out that he should probably go see the Statue of Liberty, the Staten Island Ferry, the Empire State Building, Mama Leone's Restaurant, the Twenty-One Club, the Copacabana Club, the Opera, Broadway plays, Rockefeller Center, Radio City Music Hall, and a ball game, if he had any time. He came back after a three-day trip. Folks asked, "What did you see?" He said, "All that you suggested!" Amazing—but he had just gone in and out of each place, to be able to say, "I've been there!" We'll relax and talk in Florida!

Love,
Grandpa

Lost at Sea

To Ryan:

Driving down to Florida this week, we listened to audiotapes of books. Ordinarily we favor mystery or comedy. This trip, we chose some non-fiction autobiographical survival stories. *Adrift* kept our rapt attention for the better part of two days. Stephen Callahan was a sailor who sailed a twenty-one-foot sloop. He had entered a race, trans-Atlantic Ocean, for single crew boats, starting in England. A bad storm caused many to leave the race before they reached the Canary Islands. His handcrafted, self-made sloop had an accident, leaving him alone in an inflatable rubber raft, six-passenger size, with limited food and water. More than two and a half months later, fishermen off Guadalupe Islands rescued him. He is the only person to have ever survived more than one month at sea alone in a rubber raft. His ordeals, his search for food (fish) and water (rain stills), his hallucinations, his perseverance, and his ingenuity were remarkable. How long would you last? Think about it.

Love,
Grandpa

WEDNESDAY, JULY 10, 1996

Being a Leader

To Ryan:

After our short discussion last Saturday at Bunky's regarding leaders and leadership, I thought long and hard about the subject(s). As noted, a good leader probably knows more about some things that he has to impart to others without "talking down" to them or making them feel dumb or insecure, to get their acceptance and cooperation for the task at hand. Actually, most people look to and accept another person to lead. They generally exaggerate their own shortcomings and want guidance to overcome them. A person with self-confidence, without being self-centered, can lead. A leader will have an ego but not be egotistical. A leader believes in oneself and sees success for self and team in action toward a common objective. A leader has native intelligence; listens well, thinks, anticipates, and is decisive. Ryan, picture yourself with all those attributes. You have them. Sure, a leader makes some mistakes—that's human— but then corrects and pushes on. Think about it. Try it. You'll like it, I guarantee.

Love,
Grandpa

Playing Smarter, Not Harder

To Ryan:

Thank you again for coming to our fiftieth anniversary and reunion of the Higgins clan! 'Course, everyone thanks your Uncle Rob; he put on the party with airfares, rentals, and major food. He'll be a hard act to follow when we have another big event to celebrate. Big event coming up starting this weekend: the Olympics! It's great—197 countries from all over the world competing against one another with no guns, violence, or lives lost. Have you or any of your friends thought about being in the Olympics? I never did, because I really wasn't exceptional in any sport, game, or competition. As I told you before, I'm probably a better athlete and competitor now than I was at your age. I attribute that to playing smarter, with finesse and strategy, rather than sheer power or fine-tuned skill. A lot that you do in your sports comes instinctively, because of your long hours of practice and coaching, so that you automatically react in given situations. Try to develop even more your "smarts"; play "what if" all the time. Think about it.

Love,
Grandpa

WEDNESDAY, JULY 24, 1996

Volunteering

To Ryan:

This week I'm starting another new adventure. That is, it's more a service than an adventure. I'm volunteering for an organization called SCORE, sponsored by the Small Business Administration. It stands for Service Corps of Retired Executives. During my ten years of retirement, I've done some consulting work. I got paid for that work. This is different. It's strictly volunteer; no pay in dollars and cents. However, I expect great personal satisfaction in this scenario. Entrepreneurs like your mom and Joe want to start their own business, or already have started one. To help avoid some pitfalls, to be able to talk to someone with experience in their field, and to guide to sources of greater expertise are a few of the advantages available through the SCORE organization. It's like a counseling service, rather than a consultant. It does prove one thing: it's never too late to learn more and help others. Think about it.

Love,
Grandpa

Grandma and Grandpa's Wedding

To Ryan:

Grandma and I are going out to Kay Higgins's wedding in Lake Tahoe tomorrow. That and our recent anniversary reminds me of our wedding and honeymoon. We were married in Grand Island, Nebraska. We wanted a reclusive cabin in the Colorado Mountains for our honeymoon. The evening of our wedding, we boarded a Pullman train for Denver. My brothers, Ed and Chuck, short-sheeted our upper berth on the train, but did include some leftover champagne for later. We took a bus out of Denver for Estes Park. There, we hailed a taxi for our trip to our "heavenly" retreat. As the cab driver stopped for gas on the way out of town, we figured that he needed that for our long ride up and through the mountains. He startled us with, "You can get out now. This is it." "It" was a filling station with six "cabins" in a field behind. The cabins looked about as large as outhouses. After settling in, we toasted, using big glass tumblers with chunks of ice chipped from the block in the icebox, not a refrigerator! Disappointing, but we survived!

Love,

Grandpa

Emotions

To Ryan:

Happy birthday—our thoughts were with you Sunday. Gosh, one more year and you'll be eighteen, and, by legal standards, an adult. One more year of high school, too, and, by educational standards, college-bound. Do enjoy this year; enjoy your family; enjoy your friends, male and female; enjoy your schooling; and enjoy your freedom. Those all don't sound like much, but you'll look back in years to come with emotions of pleasure. On your birthday, we were at your second cousin Kay's wedding in Lake Tahoe, California. Emotions, yes. I've always had this philosophy about emotions. Weddings, funerals, and hospitals are the most emotional times in people's lives. Typically Higgins, I get into the scene—laughing, crying, commiserating, exulting, or, in a single word, emoting. And I don't think that that's all bad. Think about it.

Love,
Grandpa

Paper Mache Sculptures

To Ryan:

Staring at me whenever I drive into our garage is a six-foot-tall man. He is a paper-mache nutcracker sculpture that I fashioned for Grandma a few years back. She collects nutcracker statues, which we bring out every Christmas. This was a bit more than she really wanted. He stands outside our front door all of December until we take down Christmas decorations. In anticipation of her birthday, January 31, and of Valentine's Day, I later made a six-foot-tall heart. It's red. On one side, it says, "Loe, I love you—Me." On the reverse side it reads, "Happy Valentine's Day." We put it out in front the first two weeks of February. I'd like to make a paper-mache full-size cow for our backyard, but I don't think she'd approve. When your mom was young, I made paper-mache cats and dogs. With paper-mache (just newspaper strips, flour, and water) a person can sculpt just about anything. Are you artistic? Try it. It's easy—it's fun.

Love,

Grandpa

WEDNESDAY, AUGUST 28, 1996

Dealing with Disappointment

To Ryan:

What a bummer! Your broken collarbone, that is. Especially since that boost from your coaches just beforehand. You've had a few days since it happened to go through a series of emotions. It's probably gone from complete despair to abject acceptance. Realize though that all is not lost. As a leader, you accept the temporary set back and go forward. You still attend practice and games. You're the team's unofficial cheerleader. You study your own team's strengths and weaknesses. You project plays, people, and plans to take advantage of the team's strengths, and to overcome the team's weaknesses, in your mind. Depending on your coaches, why not ask to be part of the coaching staff, unofficially of course? Boy, what a learning experience that could be. Coaches can always use an extra cheerful, contributing, respected leader and helping hand! Reviewing game films of your opponent's teams, or even accompanying coaching scouts to future scheduled games is a winner. Think about it.

Love,
Grandpa

Staying in Shape

To Ryan:

Grandma and I had a little spending spree last week. My golf shoes were coming apart at the seams, so we shopped and bought a new pair. Since we've decided to stay home this winter instead of going to Florida, we bought a Health Rider exercise machine for Grandma. She'll be able to keep up her activity, even in the cold, icy winter in Independence. Now she walks on alternate days while I play racquetball. We both try to keep ourselves in good shape. Years ago, I attended a YMCA conference on exercise and fitness. It was a shocker for me. Although I hadn't thought at length about it, I figured that an occasional heavy-duty work-out would last for quite a while to keep a person in good shape and good health. It was stated that even Olympic athletes lost their competitive edge if they didn't keep up their specialty regimen constantly. That startled me into my yearlong schedule of handball, racquetball, golf, tennis, and exercise. Think about it.

Love,
Grandpa

Creating Your "Signatures"

To Ryan:

Do you have a signature? Of course you do! Is it readable? You're thinking about a written signature, aren't you? I'm talking about other types of individual actions, words, and characteristics that you immediately associate with certain people. Some are suitable; others are bold and exaggerated. Some carry a message; others are mere idiosyncrasies of a certain person. For instance, my famous, "It ain't what is, but what people think it is," became my "signature" phrase to all my associates I worked with over the years. A signature can be a favorite saying, as that was, to carry a message to look beyond words for meaning or interpretation. My wearing of bow ties was just a whim to be different, perhaps to appear to be more sophisticated. People now recognize me by my bow tie "signature." Same with my carrying and spending only two-dollar bills. Another "signature," perhaps my most recognized, is my starting all my speeches with the "It's a beautiful day in Independence, Milwaukee, Zanesville, or whatever city I am in," phrase. Think about it.

Love,

Grandpa

Finding a Spy

To Ryan:

While reminiscing with some old friends lately, I told them an interesting war story that happened in Europe during World War II. A friend of mine, a pilot, went to Italy with his crew as a replacement. The B-24 Bomb Group had lost ten ships and crews during the prior few months. The planes had taken off on bombing missions. About the time their landing gear was being retracted, the plane would blow up. One plane and crew lost; a week later another; a couple days later another, until ten had been destroyed: ten B-24s and one hundred airmen. About that time, the executive finance officer took his suspicions to the commanding officer. They acted quickly. The line chief (sergeant in charge of the crew chiefs of each individual plane—that is, mechanics) was called in to explain why he had sent home $1,000 after each "accident." After questioning, he admitted that he had taken German spy money ($1,000 per plane). Before each mission, his job was to inspect all planes. He would plant a demolition bomb in the locking device of the landing gear. Before the men could get to him, they court-martialed and shot him!

Love,
Grandpa

WEDNESDAY, OCTOBER 2, 1996

Pros and Cons

To Ryan:

In my new work in SCORE counseling people starting their own business, it brings back old memories. I guess everyone, at one time or another, thinks about going into business for themselves. I know that I did, more than once! A combination of hearing and investigating about a business for sale, or of starting a new one at a time when my corporate job had lost its challenge, led me to considering other avenues of endeavor. These new scenarios ranged from manufacturing bows and arrows to producing nails, to having a string of laminating machine booths at airports and malls, to introducing our own line of bow ties, to even being a manufacturer rep selling Bridgeport lathes. I'd put together a business plan with numbers for sales, expenses, and profit in great detail. I'd put down the pros and cons on the business from every angle. In all cases, the potential problems overrode the advantages. That, together with a timely promotion and pay raise from my current employer, stopped my dreaming.

Love,
Grandpa

An Addendum . . .

To Ryan:

Way to go on your collarbone recovery and getting back into the ball game with the team! 'Course, you know that Grandma and I have been with you in our prayers for your good health and speedy recovery. Wish we could be with you this weekend for Homecoming. Know that we are, in spirit. Perhaps later this year. Never will forget your catching that pass in the rain in Missoula while I was watching. Give it all you've got while you're in the game—then afterward relax and enjoy.

Love,
Grandpa

WEDNESDAY, OCTOBER 9, 1996

Buying a Business

To Ryan:

One more story on entrepreneurship from my experiences. The first number of years in corporate industrial life, while exciting, gave me some time to think of being in business by myself—or at least with one or more others in partnership. I sometimes envisioned going into business with my brothers, Ed and Chuck. Both were engineers, too. Ed would do the design and engineering; Chuck would sell; I would take care of the operations and manufacturing. Trouble was, we did not have enough money to buy or build a company. So I looked elsewhere. A good friend, Bob, had inherited money, was looking for a business, and needed me. He was a musician. He brought up a soda water bottling and delivery company that was up for sale. We looked it over, saw some possibilities, and caucused to discuss it. Bob's first comment was, "It looks like I could take off three days a week to play golf!" Right there, I backed off and out of the deal! Think about it.

Love,
Grandpa

Think Positively

To Ryan:

We were shopping this week at an antique "tourist trap." There was a funny lil' book entitled *I Love Him, But . . .* Each page had a clever quip from a wife or girlfriend, citing the strange and comical anecdotes of their partner. Example: "He'll watch anything, just so there's movement on the TV screen." It's a great book. However, on consideration, I realized that the quips were all negative, however laughable. It brought to mind a song from many years ago. Its lyrics included the lines, "Accentuate the positive, eliminate the negative, latch onto the affirmative, and don't mess with Mr. In-between!" I like to think that that's my philosophy. That is reflected in my establishment of the positive in my BAR professional engineers code, which we "discussed" last March. I guess it's another way of saying, look for the good or best in every person and situation, even in tough deals, like a collarbone broken twice. Think about it.

Love,
Grandpa

WEDNESDAY, OCTOBER 23, 1996

Fun Without Electricity

To Ryan:

Wow! Yesterday it started snowing, after a lil' rain. Not unusual in itself, albeit early in the year. Big, wet snowflakes fell. Since none of the trees had lost their leaves, the snow started accumulating and bending the branches to the ground. At 5:00 p.m. the lights went out . . . then the phone went out! Fortunately, we had an hour before it turned dark outside. We got candles and flashlights. We started the gas fireplace (with ceramic "logs"). It was cold outside, but the fire kept it livable inside. The gas furnace had electrical controls, so it was useless. We went back to Abe Lincoln's days—one-candle power! It is surprising how much light one could provide. No television, no telephone, no radio, no hot soup (electric stove, oven, and broiler all down), no heat, no electric blanket, no garage door opener (we could have opened it manually!). We cuddled in bed under a down comforter till morning, when service was returned. We empathized with the pioneers. Think about it.

Love,

Grandpa

Bill Rehnquist in High School

To Ryan:

'Tis the season for masquerade parties—Halloween, etc. That thought took me back to my high school days. We were having a masquerade party for our group of friends at the house of one of the guys in Shorewood, near Lake Drive. One of the group, driving alone in his folks' big Packard, was stopped by a policeman on Farewell Avenue, the residential area. He was asked to get out of the car. Bill, a tall young man, got out and stood beside the car in his tuxedo, with a big, wide, bright red sash crossing his chest. He was lectured by the cop about the speed limit and asked, "Did he have anything to say for himself?" Bill joined his hands in a prayerful manner and mentioned that he was on his way to a diplomatic meeting, while bending his tall frame over in supplication. To which the officer replied, "OK, this time; don't let it happen again." Bill Rehnquist, today's chief justice of the US Supreme Court, drove off in his tennis shoes!

Love,
Grandpa

WEDNESDAY, NOVEMBER 6, 1996

Making Your Vote Count

To Ryan:

Election Day yesterday—another year and you'll be able to vote. I spent about fourteen hours as an election judge again. It's great and interesting work. A little civic duty, and I get paid for it! Saw all my neighbors because I was in the neighborhood polling place for the first time. On two occasions, I had to take the ballot and voting apparatus out to the car where invalid voters were waiting to vote. As sick as they were, they were determined to vote. One vote! Some would excuse themselves with, "What does it matter, my single vote won't decide the candidate or issue in the election." 'Course, there are numerous dates in history where one vote literally changed the course of the world. Patrick Henry's resolution to defy King George's Stamp Tax passed by one vote. After the Revolution, the proposal to have German as the official language was defeated by Congress by one vote. By one vote the Senate, in 1876, agreed to purchase Alaska. In 1923, Hitler was elected leader of his party by one vote. Think about it.

Love,

Grandpa

Leadership Outside of Work

To Ryan:

One of the luxuries of retirement is the freedom to do as a person chooses . . . the ole when he wants, where he wants, how he wants, what he wants, why he wants, and with whom he wants. During my career, I felt it was obligatory to represent my company in civic, charitable, industry, and employee functions. That included joining various clubs, organizations, and associations. I really did enjoy the outside-of-work activities representing, not only the company, but also our family and myself. It led me to an interesting observation. In my opinion, I've come to believe that a person can become the president, leader, or head of any nonprofit group within a five-year, and oftentimes within a three-year, time period, after setting their mind to it! I've done it. All it took, or all it takes, was the determination, the willingness, the sacrifice, and the perseverance to do more than is expected of you, to volunteer for tasks others hesitate, refuse, or decline to do, to be willing to make decisions, and to accept responsibility. It's amazing how few people can or want to do that. Think about it.

Love,

Grandpa

Counting Your Blessings

To Ryan:

Happy Thanksgiving—tomorrow. We have so much to be thankful for; it is awesome. In anticipation, we've reviewed just a portion of the good fortune that God has bestowed on our family. I look often to ways in which I can give to others as God has given to us. I'm sure that there's more to do than we do for others and in thanksgiving to God. We'll keep trying, but I know that we'll never be able to "catch up." I've often claimed that whenever anyone feels down, put upon, discouraged, unlucky, or mad at the world for their bad luck or misfortune, that they should visit a hospital emergency room, funeral parlor, nursing home, or prison. "If only I'd done something different, sooner, later, or not at all, I wouldn't be here", has been said many times over to me in some of those locations. "How soon we get old, how late we get smart." Think about it.

Love,
Grandpa

The Coast Guard Academy

To Ryan:

My trip on the NCAA drug-testing program took me to New Jersey the weekend before Thanksgiving. It was the Division III championship football game. It was University of New Jersey (formerly Trenton State) versus Coast Guard Academy. Great game. Coast Guard scored their final touchdown with a minute remaining, a point behind. What to do? Go for the tie with the PAT, or for the win with a two-point play? They elected the PAT and missed, ending the game seventeen to sixteen. Wow, what second thoughts—going for two and failing would have been a valiant loss, but missing the "sure thing" PAT was a bummer. Nonetheless, I was impressed with the Coast Guard team and other men and women cadets attending the game. They were disciplined, respectful, and class acts. I "saw" you out there as safety for the Coast Guard team, which didn't look a lot different from your Bozeman High team. Ever consider the Coast Guard Academy? You fit their profile! They'd like to have a three-letter, three-sport jock who has brains and leadership abilities, who could transfer to SEALS afterward! Think about it.

Love,
Grandpa

WEDNESDAY, DECEMBER 11, 1996

The Impact of a First Job

To Ryan:

Recently there was an article written about corporate CEOs and the first jobs they ever had. That is, it was the first paying job they had outside the family connection, like household chores for allowances. You can't imagine the wide variety, and all of them declared that it was from some of their humble, dirty, slaving, menial, or service works that they derived lessons, attributes, and disciplines that lasted their entire working career. A sense of humor and compassion crept into the scenarios, too. I've related my first job as a paperboy to this thinking. When I sat back and thought about my list of subsequent jobs, I surprised myself. After paperboy came soda jerk, and then delivery boy on a bicycle at a drug store. At sixteen, with a driver's license, I worked as a pastry truck driver and "gofer" in a bakery store chain. Then, at eighteen, I became eligible to sign on as a "common laborer," with union wages and a card. During college—postwar—I was a carpenter with a union card, and a freelance painter.

Love,
Grandpa

Business Travel

To Ryan:

In anticipation of our trip this summer, I sought out my passport. It hasn't been used for over ten years and consequently must be renewed. This will be my fourth passport. The first trip overseas was during the war, 1945, and no passport was necessary! Then a long dry spell before your mom and Uncle Rob went over on a Rotary exchange student program, and we went over to pick them up and do a three-week tour of Europe in 1965. After college, and two companies who didn't require foreign travel, it was Allis-Chalmers "time." Looking back at my old passports, I identified seven years of business overseas trips. Most times, it was checking on supplies in Spain. A few were to South America, searching for an affiliation with an agricultural equipment manufacturer. The rest were as part of the host team of Allis-Chalmers, for dealers' awards travel to Spain and Venezuela. Now to get my shots, visa, and passport!

Love,
Grandpa

WEDNESDAY, DECEMBER 25, 1996

Playing Santa

To Ryan:

Merry Christmas! The month of December was more a month of thanksgiving for me than preparation and celebration of Christmas. This month took me into homes, rooms, and halls playing Santa Claus for people ages one to eighty-one. What an experience. If only I could have given each person what he or she wanted and asked for from Santa. Not only age difference, but material well-being separated the groups of ten to four hundred. The awe in the eyes of the innocent believers delighted me (as it did their parents). The acceptance and visible relaxation of the tough teenagers rewarded me. The smiles and welcomes from bed-ridden, seriously ill elderly patients made my day. It didn't take expensive gifts or outlandish promises to bring the holiday spirit into people's lives. I felt blessed to be able to bring some joy and happiness, however short-lived, into their world.

Love,
Grandpa

To: Ryan –

To: Ryan –

MEMORANDUM

About once a year contact lenses should be replaced. It's my time. Last week I had a regular eye exam and ordered new contacts. I'd really like to have a laser operation so that I could forego glasses of any kind. They haven't perfected it for far-sighted as the...

...an –

MEMORANDUM

...same time that I read Tiger Woods... came across Bill Gates story in...

MEMORANDUM

same...

To: Ryan –

MEMORANDUM

Thank you for your note. You don't ... o their... not need to repay me. Instead, quote: Parents (and grandparents!) expect their children (or grandchildren) to repay them for their upbringing by being good to their own children (grandchildren or grandparents got from all that gobbledegook – children/grandchildren and will we in full! Ah, but on to the decision of my personal life,

---

To: Ryan –

MEMORANDUM

We had an opportunity last week to attend a dinner where the guest speaker was Johnny Bench former Cincinnati Reds All-Star catcher. I always find it fascinating to hear speakers who were formerly jockes. You get to realize that they are ordinary folks who have been endowed with God given talent.

1997

WEDNESDAY, JANUARY 1, 1997

Betting on Horse Races

To Ryan:

Happy New Year! How great it was to see you at Aunt Barb's for the Higgins Christmas celebration. You're looking good. Fortunately, the cards were running my way in our singles games, and our way in our couple's victories in gin. Do you play cribbage? We'll try that next time. During my last NCAA drug testing trip to New Jersey, one of the crew and I went to Atlantic City during our off time. I lost my usual twenty dollars on the slots. My partner hit it big (big to me is about $300 or $400), while I talked to one of the "pit bosses" at the crap table. Next casino visit, I'm going to try his method. Hooks me back to the time Uncle Rob went with us to the horse races in Omaha. All the way driving up there, he noticed sign boards, highway signs, and license plates in combinations of the number seven. He felt it was a sign, a signal, or a premonition on betting. Sure enough, he put down bets all afternoon on seven. He was ahead by the last race, so he bet all his money on seven in the last race. It came in second! Uncle Rob said that he probably would have become addicted, had he won! Think about it.

Love,
Grandpa

Tiger Woods

To Ryan:

Have you read the *Sports Illustrated* issue with the Sportsman of the Year on the cover, Tiger Woods? His and his father and mother's story is an amazing six or eight pages of a phenomenal account of a family. Do get it and read it. It encompasses not only an athlete's bringing up but also the complete devotion of two dedicated parents and the ethnic overtones of being Chinese, Indian, African American, and Thai, and yet being outcast as a "black" man. A lot of disciplines, respect, mind-sets, philosophy, prejudices, and victories to think about as I read the tale. It reminded me of my old saying: "If I weren't an Irish Catholic, I'd probably be an Oriental Jew!" My reasoning being that Orientals have such great family closeness, discipline, respect, perseverance, and work ethic, and Jews have such intensity, persistence, religion, family, work ethic, and cultural and educational goals. I believe in all of the above.

Love,
Grandpa

Preparing to Interview

To Ryan:

Sources tell me that you will be visiting more than one college campus in your quest for the best spot for you to continue your education—formal education, that is. That means interviewing with the professors, coaches, and administrators. That means dressing up (Boston Celtics always wear jackets and ties in traveling), standing and sitting up straight during meetings, a firm handshake and easy smile on introduction, loud and clear answers on questioning, and rehearsed and concise statements on accomplishments and goals, with a sprinkling of sincere yes sir or ma'am and no sir or ma'am thrown in to complete the good impression. Do you know that I dressed up for classes during my entire last semester in college? It was to get me feeling comfortable for upcoming interviews and jobs. I practiced answers to expected questions with Grandma at night before those interviews. The preparation paid off. Think about it.

Love,
Grandpa

More Random Acts of Kindness

To Ryan:

About the same time that I read Tiger Woods's story, I came across Bill Gates's story in Time magazine. As president of Microsoft, his influence has been far-reaching. He didn't finish college, either, but each left school to pursue their own God-given talents. While I enjoy reading books, I find that biographies are even more fascinating than my other favorite—mysteries. Recently, I picked up a book at a garage sale along those lines. It's over forty years old, but the background involves the same perseverance, ingenuity, and hard work that Gates and Woods display. I'll send it to you when I finish. Any RAKs lately? I have to share one with you. Grandma and I were eating dinner at a buffet. We noticed a mother and four kids. The twelve-year-old son was especially helpful to his mom with his younger sisters and brother. It so impressed his mom, and us, that we offered and bought their dinner. Think about it.

Love,
Grandpa

Preparing for the Trip to Africa

To Ryan:

Received my passport this week. Get yours yet? Or are we going outside the USA? I'm kidding. You have plenty of time to settle on our destination, trip, and itinerary. An article in this week's local paper conjured up some background information and fantasy on archaeology—Israel is close to Egypt. A Rotary friend of mine recently returned from Egypt. He has some videos, books, and brochures to prepare travelers. He said that there are four points to be sure to see, if a person visits Egypt. First is the Egyptian Museum, then the Sphinx, then the Pyramids, and, lastly, the Valley of Kings or Luxor Valley. Have you done any research on the trip? I'll be checking the next month or so about shots before venturing outside the country. I wonder if we'll have to get visas for our travel. The travel agent should know all those type answers

Love,

Grandpa

Johnny Bench and Teamwork

To Ryan:

We had an opportunity last week to attend a dinner where the guest speaker was Johnny Bench, former Cincinnati Reds All-Star catcher. I always find it fascinating to hear speakers who were formerly jocks. You get to realize that they are ordinary folks who have been endowed with God-given talents. He spoke well. His message centered on teamwork. He cited the vowels of teamwork: "A" is for attitude, necessary for all members to subjugate self; "E" is for effort, everyone to give their all to the best of ability; "I" is for individuality, to bring out the special talents of each one to mesh with the others; "O" is for opportunity, to take advantage of that given by opponents as well as making your own; and "U" is for using people to accomplish a useful, successful objective for the team. Put them all together, and they spell teamwork and success.

Love,
Grandpa

WEDNESDAY, FEBRUARY 12, 1997

Lincoln and Perseverance

To Ryan:

Talking with some friends about the time that I was "doing" Santa Claus in December, someone suggested that I'd make a better Abe Lincoln. I'd thought of that before. He was tall, lanky, and persevering—like me! At age twenty-two, Abe failed in business. At twenty-three, he was defeated in a race for the Illinois Legislature. Next year, he failed again in business. Finally, at twenty-five, he was elected a legislator. Then his sweetheart died the next year, which contributed to his nervous breakdown the following year. At twenty-nine, he was defeated for Speaker, at thirty-one defeated for elector, and at thirty-four defeated for Congress. Three years later, he won, but then lost his seat in Congress two years after that. At forty-six, he ran and lost a race for senator; was defeated for vice president at forty-seven; and again defeated for a Senate seat two years later. Then, guess what—at fifty-one he was elected president of the United States. Talk about courage, persistence, and perseverance! Keep plugging away—you, too, will be rewarded.

Love,

Grandpa

Lent and Ash Wednesday

To Ryan:

Last Wednesday was Ash Wednesday, wasn't it? The ash cross on the forehead to remind us of our mortality. We all eventually "return" to dust. I guess that our New Year's Resolutions sort of overlap with our Lenten resolves. How long are your lists? Mine are kind of short. One of my New Year's resolutions is that I "review each night my daily faults and accomplishments and next day's objectives." During Lent, I'm going to ensure that I do more "random acts of kindness." 'Course, we are abstaining from meat on Fridays, and we fasted and abstained on Ash Wednesday. A little effort, but it is some sacrifice for us during Lent. Maybe, since we're over seventy, we're not bound by these "suggestions," but it's little enough sacrifice in thanksgiving for all that God has given and bestowed on us and our family. More and more, the Church is guiding and suggesting, rather than the rigid rules of the past. Everyone is their own clergy and counselor.

Love,
Grandpa

WEDNESDAY, FEBRUARY 26, 1997

Wishbone, Backbone, and Funny Bone

To Ryan:

How's the ole collarbone? Healing well, we hope. It shouldn't bother you in track—just make sure that you land properly on your triple jump! Bones! The priest last Sunday talked about bones. That is, he said that we all have to consider our three "main" bones—our wish bone, our backbone, and our funny bone. 'Course, wishing won't make it come true, but we all have times of projecting ourselves onto situations that are ideal and desirable. It's good to wish, and then work on the stuff to make our wishes reality, with the help of family, friends, and God. Then there's the backbone—the guts to take a stand, to stick to it through adversity, criticism, or peer pressure, because you know it's right. Lastly, so we don't take ourselves too seriously, to see the fun side of life using our funny bone, we have fun. Think about it.

Love,
Grandpa

Giving Back

To Ryan:

It has been busy lately. While I never felt that I'd be bored during retirement, I never visualized having such a busy schedule. The local YMCA and Independence School District are jointly projecting a fund-raising campaign. They recruited me for the special gifts position. This post is for the wealthy movers and shakers around town. If I can extract "big bucks" from a few VIPs and companies, it is supposed to provide a challenge to the rest of the community to pitch in. We'll see. Then, they brought me back on the Community Foundation, which I helped start about fifteen years ago. I'm development committee chair, which is another way of saying "fund-raiser." It's getting more difficult to get people to donate their money to charity. To me, it's like having to pay income taxes, being able to have a job and making money—thank goodness I can pay taxes. Similarly, being healthy and wealthy—thank goodness I can share with the less fortunate. Think about it.

Love,

Grandpa

WEDNESDAY, MARCH 12, 1997

Owning a Business

To Ryan:

What experiences I'm having working for SCORE (Service Corps of Retired Executives). Being a part of big corporations all my working career sheltered me somewhat from entrepreneurs. 'Course, I searched long and hard for my own business all during those years. Never found one, largely because I'd do a "pro forma" profit-and-loss balance sheet on a business that I wanted to start or buy, taking into account all the scenarios that could affect it, and dropped the idea. Since all that could affect it probably wouldn't come to pass, others pursued the same "dream" and were successful. One recent SCORE client came to me for counseling on his invention. On questioning, he didn't know the cost, selling price, customer base, or supplier group, but he just "knew that he was going to make a mint with it!" Another client, already in business, was lamenting the fact that he had not stashed some funds for unexpected events. He and his wife downsized their home, car, vacations, and activities in order to pay off his debts and stay in business. Think about it.

Love,
Grandpa

Mentors in Business

To Ryan:

Everyone has a mentor in business. That is, whether it is acknowledged to be or not, everyone has someone that they look up to and emulate, consciously or only in one's mind. That changes occasionally, most often from job to job or company to company. I learned a lot from my mentors. One characteristic was fascinating with one of my first bosses. I was his assistant, and then succeeded him as plant manager. As his assistant, I could study him in various scenarios. Staff members would come in and present a situation calling for action. He would listen, ask some questions, and ask for a report to be made after it had been resolved. Often, the staff person would come to me and ask, "What does he think? What does he want me to do?" I didn't give them an answer, so invariably they would go out, consider the alternatives, pick perhaps the most difficult but necessary method, and do it. It was a great technique for my boss. I later found that I had to take a direct approach instead. Think about it.

Love,
Grandpa

Wednesday, March 26, 1997

Naming a Plane

To Ryan:

How are you on nicknames? Does everyone just call you Ryan? Would you believe that my nickname was "Swans Down" as a kid? Both my brothers called me that. I must have spilled some Swans Down Cake Flour, popular at the time. 'Course, in school, most everyone knew me as "Hig." And, can you imagine, Grandma was "Smitty" to all her friends when I met her during the war, her maiden name being Smith. When we left for overseas, our crew decided to nickname our B-29 "Lucky Strike." It seemed appropriate, and some expected we'd get free cigarettes from the tobacco company! Never did! Then, I made an addition to the plane. Right under my window, on the outside, I painted "Wittle Woey." Grandma Loe's little niece's pronunciation of her name came out that way. Further, in the hub, or middle of the wheel, the "stick" controlling the plane, I had "Wittle Woey" again, written on a picture of herself in the bath that Grandma had sent me to tantalize me.

Love,
Grandpa

Playing Gin Rummy

To Ryan:

You're getting to the age that I feel that I can entrust to you the details of "How to consistently win at Gin Rummy, the Higgins method." I'm kidding, but let's discuss some of the finer points, subtler points, and nuances of the game, as taught to me by your great-grandfather, my dad.

1. Always cut the deck, if offered by the dealer.
2. Always take the "up card" turned over by the dealer, or if you're dealing and your opponent chooses not to take it.
3. Always "go down" as soon as you can, for ten or less if no up card, or for the number of the up card or less if there is an up card.
4. Never throw or discard an ace, or a two, or maybe even a three, unless there is absolutely no other choice, even to the point of breaking up a high pair.
5. Always keep track of the cards that your opponent picks up to avoid later throwing a matching card or sequential card, and to help plan your own hand to avoid waiting for a card that your opponent might already have included in one of his melds.
6. Don't let yourself be talked into going down late in the game. Better to redeal than to have your opponent undercut you with his or her low count.

Love,
Grandpa

WEDNESDAY, APRIL 9, 1997

Paying Taxes

To Ryan:

It's that time again! Income tax time. I start preparing for April 15 each year about April 16 the year before. Tracking income and expenditures each month and summarizing after twelve months makes a stress-free filling-out-the-forms routine. In my working years there wasn't much to do, since the company withheld and submitted taxes during the year, and summarized at the twelve-month year's end. I often say that there wouldn't be enough jails to hold all the violators if they hadn't instituted the withholding tax system. It would be difficult to have to pay a whole year's tax at one time, human nature being what it is. Few people would or could discipline themselves to save up all during the year for that one big payment. Since retirement, the government forces us to pay an estimated tax every three months, as a "withholding" payment. It makes sense. There are enough controls, reports, and regulations to keep everyone honest and in line. Even your Uncle Rob, who is probably least scrutinized of all of us, believes in reporting everything honestly and above-board because:

1. he tells the truth, and
2. he likes to sleep well at night.

Think about it.

Love,
Grandpa

Writing in a Gratitude Journal

To Ryan:

Someone the other day told those listening about a "Gratitude Journal" that they had started. It seems that the idea is to write down, whenever it enters your mind, something that you are thankful for, be it a person, an event, a trait, or a circumstance. Be it small or large, think about it and write it down. Right now, I've got a big one to put in my book—our good health. We're in Topeka, Kansas, at the hospital. Grandma's sister, Bobye Bethell (your Aunt Barb was named after her), had a massive brain hemorrhage yesterday in Hays, Kansas. They woke us at midnight. We drove in at 2:00 a.m. this morning. She is in a coma. The doctor's prognosis is not good. However, if anyone can overcome it, it will be one of the Smith girls, Bobye. What would you put in your journal?

Love,
Grandpa

WEDNESDAY, APRIL 23, 1997

The Blindfold Test

To Ryan:

About once a year, contact lenses should be replaced. It's my time. Last week I had a regular eye exam and ordered new contacts. I'd really like to have a laser operation so that I could forego glasses of any kind. They haven't perfected it for farsighted, as they have for nearsighted people, so it'll be awhile for me. Have you ever tried the blindfold test? Have someone blindfold you, no peeking, to simulate being blind. Maybe around your house you'll make out all right. Think, or even try, with someone along to protect you from mishap, walking outside or in unfamiliar territory. It's really scary to me. I do admire a blind person who navigates in this world, albeit with a seeing-eye dog. My premise has always been, of all my senses, the one that I would most hate to lose would be my sight. Of all your five senses, which would you feel was most precious? Think about it.

Love,
Grandpa

Actions Speak Loudly

To Ryan:

Well, it's another NCAA drug testing scene. This is a so-called "year-round" session, not a championship or tourney event. We'll be doing about eighteen football and eight track athletes at Tulsa University in Oklahoma. I'll be trying a new technique observing the participants. I'm really excited about our trip. I'm making a list, checking it twice, trying to decide what's necessary and right.

On a radio show the other day, someone was discussing his book. It had to do with communications—that is, personal communicating between people. The author claims that three main characteristics are involved. He says that 60 percent is in body language, 30 percent is accomplished by tone of voice, and only 10 percent rests in the actual words spoken. That's kind of hard to believe, isn't it? Yet it follows my old saying: "Your actions speak so loudly, I can't hear what you say!" Think about it.

Love,
Grandpa

Winning and Losing

To Ryan:

Congratulations—first in the long jump to go to state! Great job! Great concentration, I'm sure, to make sure that you didn't "scratch," as we discussed. The next few weeks are going to test you, again and again. Hang in there. Do the best you can, but realize that we all love you, no matter what. Someone quoted to me the other day: "Today, we Americans tend to put too much emphasis on being cool, on being a winner in sports, on television, and in advertising campaigns. We forget what a valuable teacher losing can be. The point is to realize that it's OK to fail, provided you get back up, dust yourself off, and try again." Seems to me, you live that every track meet in your events, as opposed to runners who only get one chance to place in a race. We'll be with you in your every jump the next three to four weeks. Think about it.

Love,
Grandpa

Becoming Computer-Savvy

To Ryan:

It's surprising just what motivates people to action. A comment, a picture, a look, a smell, a taste, a touch, or an experience can change a person, causing a different direction or outlook on life. My latest isn't all that monumental, but it does involve a definite change. We've had an IBM PC for three years. Not much usage, just some lists and reports. Then, last week, our neighbor's son arrived in his mobile home, complete with computer, software, and know-how. We talked the stock market. I'm enthused. Now I'm in the process of getting our unit updated and upgraded to 64K memory, 28.8 modem, Windows 95, Quicken tax and financial programming, and the capability to fax, e-mail, and use the Internet. I'll be going from weekly posting and calculating my fifteen-week moving averages on some 150 stocks and funds, to daily online reports. Wow. Think about that.

Love,
Grandpa

WEDNESDAY, MAY 28, 1997

Making Decisions

To Ryan:

Nice graduation picture! Recently, there was a full page of male hairdos in a magazine. I cut it out to send you, and promptly lost it. My point was to discuss how you decided to have the hairstyle you currently wear. Decisions. How do we all come to decisions in our lives? One of the advantages of age and experience is that often, there are many factors from the past brought to mind that will influence and contribute to our process of making a decision. Most scenarios come from family, then school friends, and finally playmates, when we're young. After college, the business world, particularly in our chosen field, enters the picture. At times, seemingly insignificant events cause us to make a decision that literally will change our lives. How many times have you looked back and thought about how or why you made a decision, and its subsequent result? I have, both good and bad. Think about it.

Love,
Grandpa

Winning 1st at the State Track Meet

To Ryan:

First in the state of Montana in the long jump! That is sensational. I, and a host of other people in this world, have never been first in anything in any state. Congratulations! Your years of training, while maybe not specifically for track, paid off. Not knowing how your triple jump compared to your former best, your effort, and placing sixth in the state in the triple jump probably gave you an inner glow—that you were in the state finals and you gave it your best shot, too. You'll remember those contests, your exhilaration, and your accomplishments for the rest of your life. Cherish it. It all passes too quickly, and the next challenge will occupy and crowd out the recent past all too soon. We'll recount it, and hopefully you'll share those reactions with me during our upcoming trip—your story of fame.

Love,
Grandpa

WEDNESDAY, JUNE 11, 1997

Advances in Technology

To Ryan:

I have just entered the real computer age, the cyberspace. Our computer has been upgraded to the latest and greatest mode. We can go online on the Internet and the World Wide Web. We can e-mail to anywhere in the world. We can pull up data, information, pictures from art galleries, museums, libraries, newspapers, magazines, and stock markets almost instantaneously. When we are in Africa next week, we can send your mom and Grandma progress reports via e-mail. The world has gone from paper and pencil when I was in grade school, to slide rules for engineering classes when in college, to battery-operated calculators, to sunlight-generated calculators, to computers that filled buildings, to hand-held computers capable of delivering vast quantities of quality knowledge up to date in real time. Think about the advances that will develop as you get to be my age.

Love,

Grandpa

The Impact of Violence

To Ryan:

Isn't it a shame that violence has invaded our world? Other than international wars, it has come down to street muggings, drive-by shootings, and the necessity of locking the doors to our homes. It has come to the point of not knowing who to trust on just simple everyday occurrences. It's difficult, if not impossible, to pinpoint the moment, the instance, or the reasoning as to the change. I can remember as a youngster not ever having to lock our home. As a matter of fact, we couldn't find the key had we occasion to lock it, anyway. Then, too, a common house key would fit all the doors in the neighborhood. Now, besides double-bolt locks, steel bars on patio doors, and an electric motion detector monitoring system, we still rely on neighbors to watch out for us. Why? Think about it. Can we do anything to better it?

Love,
Grandpa

WEDNESDAY, JUNE 25, 1997

Devising a New Game

To Ryan:

I've devised a new game. Perhaps misnamed a game, but a discussion vehicle nonetheless. I'm open to suggestions for a name. I like The Game! Rules are these:

1. Two or more players to start the game.
2. One person challenges another or group as to picking out to be "challenged" or "challenger."
3. The "challenger" then names a "word." The word can be a noun (preferably), a verb, an adverb, or an adjective. It could be a phrase, if needed.
4. It is then up to the "challenged" to define the meaning, i.e., that person's own opinion of the word, as expansive as desired, as diverse as wanted.
5. Then, the "challenged" must discuss various aspects, consequences, results, and variations relative to the subject.
6. On completing their discourse, the "challenged" finishes his contribution and opens it to others by announcing "discussion."

We should get some active and heated pronouncements with ensuing conversations. So much the better. Think about it.

Love,

Grandpa

Family First

To Ryan:

For the last six Wednesday letters I've decided to review my worst and best decisions on the financial, career, and personal aspects of my life. The worst financial decision I made had to do with stock transactions while I was working for a company as vice president. We had purchased one hundred shares of company stock for each of our four children, your mom being one of them. I always felt that it showed loyalty, and I expected the company to prosper, hopefully through some of my working efforts. On a takeover bid by another company, the stock tripled in price. After considering selling for the children's benefit, we declined, because I knew the president revicwed stock sales. Also, we were greedy, expecting it to go higher. Alas, it sank to about our purchase price. Other vice presidents had sold. We hadn't! I resolved to never again put company loyalty above family benefits. Think about it.

Love,
Grandpa

WEDNESDAY, JULY 9, 1997

Best Financial Decision

To Ryan:

Hey, we're home again! Great feeling, isn't it? We're to the best financial decision from my viewpoint. It had to do with stock transactions, too. As vice president at another company, I had been given stock options as another incentive to help make the company grow more profitable. They were great perks. We took advantage of the opportunity by buying into the options as the stock price rose above the option price. That required a lot of money, more than Grandma and I had available. The company had induced the bank to loan us the money to exercise the options. One day, Grandma and I talked about the huge debt that we had incurred and was now hanging over our "financial" heads. Both of us had been raised in the Depression and were therefore fiscally conservative. We decided to sell enough stock to pay off our loan completely. We did. As the stock price sank and dividends began to shrink, we thanked God for our decision. Think about it.

Love,
Grandpa

Worst Career Decision

To Ryan:

I think that I am fully recovered from our trip. From your e-mail from Bozeman, it sounds like you are, too. We'll have many memories to reminisce about for years to come. This letter brings me to another decision story, my worst career decision. 'Course, often it's a long time before we realize that we made a poor decision "back when." Such is the case here. After the World War II experience as a bomber pilot, with an MOS (military occupational status) accordingly, I determined that while I enjoyed flying, in the next conflict I didn't want to get shot at again. So I changed my MOS to "purchasing and production control officer." I figured that I would be safe behind a big, brown desk, about six thousand miles "behind the lines" of war. Also, it followed what I was doing in my job after graduating from Cornell. Then I decided to resign my commission because I didn't want summer camp and one weekend per month training. Big mistake. I could enjoy a colonel's pension and perks now. Think about it.

Love,
Grandpa

WEDNESDAY, JULY 23, 1997

Best Career Decision

To Ryan:

It's about my best career decision time now. That is a difficult decision in itself—that is, deciding which of the many options I had to choose from during my working life and career. After reviewing my list of possible candidates, I've chosen one as the best. First, let's review the list: where to concentrate—sports or studying; which college—Cornell or Lehigh; what engineering—mechanical, electrical, civil, or chemical; what discipline post college—marketing, engineering, or manufacturing; which company—Line Material, Ford, or DuPont; how long to stay at a company— one year, five years, a lifetime, or as long as they challenge me; when to move within a company—South Milwaukee or Zanesville; who to work for after the first company— George J. Meyer or Allis-Chalmers; which management technique to take as your identity—by the book, interpretive, or visionary. There were many more, but my best career decision was choosing Cornell.

Love,
Grandpa

Worst Personal Decision

To Ryan:

Thank you for your note. You don't owe me a thing, nor need to repay me. Instead, let me quote: parents and grandparents should only expect their children or grandchildren to repay them for their upbringing by their children being good to their own children, the parents' grandchildren, or grandparents' great-grandchildren. From all that gobblegook—be good to your children and grandchildren, and you'll have "paid" me in full!

Ah, but on to the worst decision of my personal life, as promised. I have undoubtedly made many bad decisions, too numerous to recall. However, many of those might have been a non-happening if I had not made what I now consider the worst decision in my personal life. I was lazy. I had many excuses, alibis, and reasons as to why I couldn't do the work, attend the meetings, or exercise the discipline necessary to complete the task. That decision was to not pursue the job of becoming an Eagle Scout. Think about it.

Love,
Grandpa

WEDNESDAY, AUGUST 6, 1997

Best Personal Decision

To Ryan:

Happy birthday on Monday. Wow, you're now eighteen! May you get everything you deserve, and deserve everything that you get. With this, the last Wednesday letter you'll receive, since you're now eighteen, let me close with this thought: When you're in a situation where you're wondering, "What should I do?" remember my adaptation of the saying, "What would Jesus do?"—that is, "What would Grandpa do?" I'll be with you!

Now, to my last of the six decisions, the best decision in my personal life. That one is a snap. My best decision in my personal life was to marry Grandma Loe. That may sound trite, but she has endured so many of my failings, my ego trips, my highs, and my lows. She has been a beautiful woman all her life in physical, mental, and psychological ways. How many seventy-four-year-old women can compare to her in all those? I hope and pray that you find a mate equal to her. All my love to you and your future.

Love,
Grandpa

Afterword

Twelve years later, Ryan decided to respond in kind
to his Grandpa. Here's his first letter:

Grandpa,

Ashley and I went to Bozeman this past Thanksgiving and
spent time with Mom and Joe. While we were there, I reread
the book *The Wednesday Pen* that Mom printed from your
letters.

In high school, when you wrote them to me, they
were neat stories that I enjoyed reading, but my own self-
centeredness and immaturity never allowed me to truly
appreciate them.

When I read the book, I felt a lot of pride in who my
grandfather is, and the stories you shared with me and,
thanks to mom, the rest of the family. As a Christian,
married, almost thirty-year-old man, I finally understood
everything you wrote me. A lot of things you taught me
when I was young stuck with me as I got older.

Leadership and hard work were things you would tell
me about, and, as I read the letters again, I realized you were

still always teaching me about them. I wanted you to know that they are two pillars in my life.

One thing I realized is that I talked to you a lot more when I was an adolescent. Both of our lives have changed since those times. There are things about me I would like to tell you. Not selfish or prideful stuff, but times where I saw the truth of your wisdom.

Now you are one of the smartest men I know personally, but a man is never too old to learn something new, even from his grandson . . .

So I would like to write you letters now. It will give us a way to reconnect, and God has been putting it in my heart ever since I read the book at Thanksgiving. Monday will be our day, and I will e-mail your account. I figure times have changed since you handwrote my letters, so I will use technology accordingly. That way, no matter where I am, I will always be able to reach you.

Love,
Ryan

About the Author

Warren Higgins was born August 8, 1924, in Kenosha, Wisconsin, where his father was city attorney and his mother owned a boutique. Warren grew up in Milwaukee, where his great-grandfather, William Strothman, was the first German settler there. After customary grade and high schools, he attended Cornell University in Ithaca, New York, on a McMullen Scholarship in mechanical engineering.

World War II was on during his freshman year when Warren enlisted as an army aviation cadet. He was called up in February 1943. After pilot training, he was commissioned and prepared to take his own B-17 crew to England. However, he was reassigned to B-29s at Grand Island, Nebraska. As copilot, Warren flew the "Lucky Strike" under Captain Bob Rodenhouse. As a result of four of the five fire raids over Japan within a nine-day period, he and his crew were awarded the Distinguished Flying Cross. Following eleven missions, Warren transferred to the "Reamatroid," under Captain Ed Russell. That crew was picked for lead crew training at Muroc Field in California, returning to Tinian Island in the Pacific after that training. They stayed based there until the war's end. During his air force career, Lieutenant Higgins was also awarded the Air Medal with three oak leaf clusters.

Warren reentered Cornell and graduated in February 1949. He spent his executive career in engineering and manufacturing at three companies serving the electrical, beverage, and agricultural industries. He retired in 1986 as vice president and general manager at the Deutz-Allis Company in Independence, Missouri.

Warren married Loe Jane Smith in Grand Island in 1946 and had four children: Rob, Ris, Charlie, and Barb. His first grandchild was Ryan, for whom he wrote *The Wednesday Pen.* After Loe's death in 1999, he renewed a friendship with a long-standing family friend, Maxine Murphy, and they married in 2001. That marriage expanded his family by three more children—Scott, Brian, and Mara—and four more grandchildren. In 2011 Warren and Max became great-grandparents when Ryan and his wife, Ashley, welcomed Penelope into the world.

The previous bio is a typical one, full of interesting information about the man who wrote all the Wednesday letters. However, there is a vitality to his life that must be added to fully appreciate how Warren contributes to his family and his community:

Warren has been an active Rotarian since 1959, and, while serving as president, started every single Rotary meeting with, "It's a beautiful day in Zanesville!" He has served on bank and hospital boards and helped start a community foundation in his perennial spirit of giving back to each of the communities in which he has lived.

I remember going to the YMCA every Saturday as a kid while my dad played handball and racquetball, sports he continued for forty-five years. When he was seventy-seven, he participated in a senior triathlon, and now keeps his golf game on.

Upon his retirement, my brother Charlie gave Dad his own Santa Claus suit, which he gleefully wore to dozens of events, sharing his good cheer. Even today, during the Christmas holidays, he wears a Santa Claus hat and jams his coat pockets with small candy canes to pass out to everyone he encounters.

In 2009, during the bicentennial of Abraham Lincoln's birth, Dad dressed his six-foot-two-inch frame in a black top hat with a Lincoln-esque black riding coat, dyed his white hair black, and spent the day at local schools talking with kids about Lincoln. Before he showed up at the schools, he stopped at a bank and picked up rolls of Lincoln-head pennies to pass out to the kids.

My two favorite legacies of my dad have to do with his role as grandpa. The first highlights his commitment and love to each grandchild. Upon the birth of each of his original eight grandchildren, this busy vice president found the time to cross-stitch an heirloom-quality quilt as a gift for each grandchild. The second legacy stretches my own sense of generosity. My dad decided that, as each grandchild reached eighteen years of age and graduated from high school, he would take them on the trip of their choice anywhere in the world. My two sons had the pleasure and honor of traveling with their grandpa to Africa. Ryan decided to go to Egypt, Tanzania, and Kenya. Seven years later, Brandon traveled to South Africa, Zimbabwe, Namibia, and Botswana with his grandpa.

In 2009 my dad turned eighty-five and thought it might be best to have his four kids accompany the remaining six grandchildren on their trips. He gave us all a budget and one other stipulation: each grandchild has to go on their trip with an aunt—my sister or myself—or an uncle—one of my two brothers—instead of their parent. It was my dad's way of enhancing the experience.

He keeps his life vital, which adds to all of ours. Even today, whenever he speaks to community groups, he hands out his card with the title "American Patriot and Veteran."

When he finishes speaking and the spirit moves him, he leads the group in singing "God Bless America." What's not to love about that?

—Ris A. Higgins